History of Douglas School
Winchester, Virginia

A Tribute to
Endurance, Belief,
Perseverance, and Success

DOUGLAS SCHOOL
KW⊞ 80

History of Douglas School
Winchester, Virginia

A Tribute to
Endurance, Belief,
Perseverance, and Success

Judy Humbert and June Gaskins-Davis
with the collaboration of Rebecca Ebert, Bettina Helm, and Capricia Shull

Winchester–Frederick County Historical Society, Winchester, Virginia
2014

Winchester-Frederick County Historical Society
1340 S. Pleasant Valley Road
Winchester, Virginia 22601
www/winchesterhistory.org

Individual photographs can be ordered through the Stewart Bell Jr. Archives in the Handley Regional Library at archives@handleyregional.org.

Printing: CreateSpace.com

Cover by The 1717 Design Group, Inc.

ISBN # 1502429063

To the teachers, staff, students, parents, and community members who worked together to create at Douglas School an environment of educational excellence, endurance, faith, and perseverance that led to student success in academics, sports, music, and life.

ALMA MATER

HAIL DOUGLAS HAIL

Down in the valley, where apple blossoms bloom,
Stands our Alma mater, brave and true,
Hail Douglas, Hail, Hail, Hail, long may thy ideals stand.
Firm o'er Virginia's land, for ever more.

How can I forget thee. The Jewel of my heart,
I'll wear thy memory, and never part,
When Spring and flowers fade, The Sun sets in the West
Your memory will come, and give me rest.

Oh, when the time shall come, the Best of friends must part,
I'll carry thy fond remembrance in my heart,
Oh, Alma mater, Thy colors white and blue,
Wave on Old Douglas, For ever more

Words by: Ellsworth Turner
Class of 1932

Music: Thuringian Folk Song

CONTENTS

FOREWORD

The Winchester-Frederick County Historical Society is honored to publish *History of Douglas School, Winchester, Virginia: A Tribute to Endurance, Belief, Perseverance, and Success.* This is the first book to document the history of Douglas School, which served the African American community from the day it opened in 1878 until the integration of the Winchester public school system in 1966. In the text and photographs of Douglas's teachers and students, sports teams and graduating classes, we see a dedication to learning and to friends and family that continues to inspire us.

Douglas School is beloved by all who attended and remember it, and this book is a testimony to its place in our community. It has been made possible through the efforts of two alumni—June Gaskins-Davis and Judy Humbert. For more than a decade they have collected photographs, school documents, and some forty years of memories. With the collaboration of Rebecca Ebert, archivist at the Handley Regional Library, they have searched newspapers and school records. Capricia Shull spent many long hours working with text and pictures to achieve a balanced, beautiful book that will be a delight to have. Their project now gives us a permanent record of Douglas School, advancing our understanding of the past and affirming its meaning for our collective future.

George Schember
President, Winchester-Frederick County Historical Society

ACKNOWLEDGMENTS

Douglas School was the heart and center of the African-American community of Winchester and Frederick County, Virginia, during the days of segregation from 1878 to 1966 when the doors at Douglas were closed as an all black school. Douglas was also vital to the students of Frederick County, Strasburg and Woodstock communities in Shenandoah County as their students rode school buses into Winchester each day for high school. All of these communities were very supportive of the students and activities at Douglas.

Fellowship and reminiscences continue with the Douglas Alumni Association from 1934 to the present day. There was a growing interest to document the story of accomplishments and pride for future generations. Judy Humbert and June Gaskins-Davis, graduates of Douglas, were persuaded to undertake this task. Former students, faculty, and staff, connected with the school, shared their photographs, items, news articles, and memories for this book.

The Winchester School Board minutes, *The Winchester Evening Star*, city directories, census records and court records were searched to provide details. Archives Room staff Rebecca Ebert, Jerry Holsworth, and Joan Wood assisted with research. Bettina Helms did an outstanding job scanning photographs and preparing captions. Volunteers Nancy Lee Comer and Marianne Argall edited and prepared material for use. We appreciate the volunteers who read the *Winchester Star* and pulled articles about Douglas School. Charles Harris of the Douglas Alumni Association shared photographs he had collected from reunions that were held over the years. Jimmy Dix shared material compiled on the Barksdale years of the athletic department.

Many thanks to all who assisted with providing identification for as many people as possible. Donations received from Dr. Andrew Gaskins aided in the preparation of photographs for this project. We offer grateful appreciation to the Winchester-Frederick County Historical Society for publishing this book. Capricia Shull and Robert Grogg took the lead in preparing our manuscript for the printers.

Many thanks to all who assisted with providing identification for as many people as possible. Donations received from Dr. Andrew Gaskins aided in the preparation of photographs for this project. We offer grateful appreciation to the Winchester-Frederick County Historical Society for publishing this book. Capricia Shull and Robert Grogg took the lead in preparing our manuscript for the printers.

We are indebted to all who have contributed to this book. We have told the story as completely and accurately as we could, based on the material we were able to locate. These chapters, by no means, include everything that happened at Douglas nor does it give every detail. Those mentioned are just to spark a memory of good times with fellow classmates and teachers. Much of this information is taken from articles published in the *Winchester Star*. The reporters were students from Douglas. The entire articles are on file in the Stewart Bell Jr. Archives located in the Handley Library. We urge you to visit the archives "to get the rest of the story."

If you have additional photographs and stories, please share them with the Stewart Bell Jr. Archives of the Handley Regional Library and the Winchester Frederick County Historical Society. They will be added to the Douglas Alumni Association Collection and will be available for future endeavors.

Judy Humbert & June Gaskins-Davis
November 2014

THE BEGINNING

EDUCATION 1871-1966

Page Hall and Powell W. Gibson seated on steps of Old Stone Presbyterian Church School, c. 1916. The school became known as Douglas School under the leadership of Powell Gibson in 1916. (204-80)

In old Mount Carmel Free Will Baptist Church, soon after the Civil War, the first school for colored people was organized. Reverend Burrell and Miss Laura Hall formed the first faculty. The task proved a hard one for Reverend Burrell, who gave up his position as principal after one year of service. He was succeeded by Professor Murray who served for two years and then passed the job along to Professor Georg Stevens a Hampton graduate, who brought order out of disorder and did splendid work.

The move to establish a public school for the black residents of the area can be traced to January 5, 1871, when the minutes of the Winchester School Board state that "a committee was formed to confer with the most prominent colored persons of the town to ascertain whether competent teachers can be employed here and to ascertain what school rooms can be rented and other information as will be necessary to get the school underway by the of February next."

Planning must not have worked out as easily as had been hoped, for it was not until May 31, 1875, that an agreement was drawn up between John Linn, trustee for the Old School Congregational Baptist Church, and the Winchester School Board. The church leased the building to the school board for ninety-nine years for the sum of one dollar. The structure was to be used as a free school for the black children of Winchester. The agreement charged the school board with making the necessary repairs to turn the building into a school and of maintaining it once it was in operation. The school board minutes of May 17, 1878, show the repairs totaled $446, not an inconsequential sum in those days.

Students first met in the Old Stone Presbyterian Church building for classes in 1878. The building was divided into three rooms and was heated by a wood stove. Older boys were responsible for keeping the

Opposite Page: Students gathered in front of Douglas School held at Old Stone Presbyterian Church building c. 1916. (69-3)

fire going.   The school was called the Winchester Colored School until 1916 and Professor Gibson's arrival.   The name was then changed to Douglas School to honor the black abolitionist and civil rights leader.   The only playground was Piccadilly Street.   The school went through the ninth grade. Students who wanted to continue their education had to go to Manassas to attend high school.

Douglas School students and teachers, taken outside the Old Stone Presbyterian Church building in 1924 or possibly earlier. Front row, left to right: Clark Dixon, L. Fine, John Henry Preston, Jefferson Lewis, Henry Moss Brooks, Rodman Turner; Second row, left to right: W. Long, Frances Greene, B. McPeyon, unidentified, Vdol, Magnolia A. William, Thelma Harris, Pearl Lavender, Elizabeth Cook; Third row, left to right: Charles Andrews, Sammy Ford, Harry B. Nickens, Hattie Mitchell (teacher), Howard Walker, unidentified, Annie Davis, Maggie Nickens, and Mary Bell Davis. (599-56)

COLORED PEOPLE EXPRESS THANKS

At a special meeting of the colored citizens of Winchester, representing four colored congregations assembled in mass meeting on February 7 in St. Paul's A.M. E. Church, the following resolutions were adopted by a unanimous vote:

"Resolved. That we, the colored citizens of Winchester, do hereby acknowledge and appreciate the magnificent gift of the benefactor, Judge Handley, in bequesting to us a legacy of so vast importance, and in the same spirit we tended our heartfelt thanks and appreciation to the Handley Board of Trustees and to the City School Board, for the interest they are manifesting to give us the improvements so much needed educationally.

"Resolved. That we take this means to publicly thank you for what has been done."

M. Armstead Chairman of Committee

Winchester Evening Star
Feb. 27, 1919

P. W. GIBSON'S

NEW

DRAMA

By
Students
of the
Douglass
School

FRIDAY NIGHT, FEB. 11, 1921
"The King of the Mandingoes"

Three American officers in the service of Liberia, Africa, decide, while on a furlough, to search for several missionaries who have been isolated in the jungles for several years. The mysterious native guide, who accompanies the officers into the land of the Mandingoes, finally proves to be the rightful king.

CAST

Twain	The King
Scragga	The Princess
Umbopa	The Mysterious Guide
Foulata	Who is to be sacrificed to the gods
Gogoola	The Prophetess
Infados	The Chief

Col. Young		Grace
Maj. Ballard	American Officers	Portia — American Missionaries
Capt. Brown		Florence

Witch Doctors, Flower Girls, Warriors.

ADMISSION 15c

Douglas School children in costume for "King of the Mandingoes," a play written by Powell W. Gibson and performed by the children on February 11, 1921. The school was then located at the Old Stone Presbyterian Church, 306 East Piccadilly Street. Front row left to right: Violet Tokes, Viola Finley, Nannie Gaskins, George Washington Callen, Hester Tokes, Ruth ____, unidentified, Lawrence Meyers, ____Carter. Second row center left to right: Helen Jennings,____Harris, ____ Lupton, Maria Conley,____Carter. Third row left to right: Virginia Green,Katheleen Banks, Hazel Green, Joe Long,Walter Carter, George Nickens, Jasper Brown, Pocahontas Jackson, Mary____, Tessie Finley. Fourth row left to right: Julian "Jute" Myers, Kenneth Bell, Powell Willard Gibson Jr., Carl Long, Madison Jennings, Lucille Hogans. (1076-25)

Powell W. Gibson, in doorway, with students at Douglas School held at the Old Stone Presbyterian Church building; date unknown. (1493-3)

Powell W. Gibson (back row, center) with teachers and class at Douglas School held at Old Stone Presbyterian Church building. c.1920. (1493-2)

COLORED SCHOOL TO GET LIBRARY

The Handley Trustees and the School Board have developed a cooperative plan whereby a branch of the Handley Library has been opened in the Douglas Colored School. About five hundred books have been set aside exclusively for the use of this library, which it is hoped will grow into an organization large enough to warrant the establishment of a library for colored people in the new school building that is to be built on the Smithfield farm property.

The Douglas branch of the Handley Library will be opened every week-day afternoon from 4 to 6 o'clock, and on Tuesday, Thursday and Saturday evenings from 7 to 9 o'clock. Reading room matter will be provided, as well as reference books and books for circulation.

Hattie Mitchell, one of the teachers in the Douglas School, will serve as librarian, having studied the duties of her position under the direction of Mr. Vernon Eddy, the Handley Librarian.

By this arrangement-the colored people of this city will have their own exclusive room, reference and circulation books and it is hoped that the patronage of this branch library will justify adding to the equipment.

Winchester Evening Star
October 1, 1921

Students in front of Old Stone Presbyterian Church when it was used as Douglas School. c. 1920s. Front row, left to right, unidentified, unidentified, John Triplett, John Carl Greene, Rodman Turner, James Stephenson, Ellsworth Turner, unidentified; Second row, unidenfied,_____ Jackson, Lilly Greene, Bertha Myers, Annie Turner, Gertrude Turner, Anna Brooks, unidentified, Frances Lee Finley, Alberta Jackson, unidentified, Lucille Carter; Third row, Tralice Dixon, unidentified, unidentified, Blanche Gibson, Moten (teacher), unidentified, Lucille Finley, unidentified, and unidentified. (1493-162)

Students at Douglas School The only two positive identifications are Nannie Gaskins, 3rd from left) and Pocahontas Jackson, 4th from left. No year given. 555-147

4th and 5th grade students attending classes at Mt. Carmel Baptist Church. Left to right (front row): Virginia Swift, Catherine Green, Florence Shelton, unidentified, Gertrude Brooks; (2nd row) Preston Jackson, Irving DIxon, Sylvia Tralice Dixon, Sadie Amelia Finley, Ruth Drummond, Joe Willis, Arthur Gaither; (back row) Germain Ford, Paul James, Anna Q. Brooks [Tokes] (teacher), Phillip Washington. (599-52)

The superintendent presented a plan to rent the basement of Mt. Carmel Free Will Baptist Church for the sum of $20.00 for eight months to be used as a schoolroom for the colored children. This was to help with the overcrowding at the Piccadilly St. School. The motion carried.

Winchester School Board Minutes
October 5, 1925

1927

THE NEW DOUGLAS SCHOOL, WINCHESTER, VA., –
GIFT OF JUDGE HANDLEY.

Douglas School at
590 North Kent
Street, Winchester,
Virginia, when newly
built in 1927. Shed
visible in front of
school held tools
and other items.
(204-43a)

New Douglas School

BOARD DECIDES ON CONSTRUCTION OF A NEW SCHOOL

By the 1920s, the three-room school was no longer suitable nor an acceptable environment for learning. In 1924 there were 183 students in attendance at the Old Stone Church, three-quarters of whom were forced into half-day shifts due to the insufficient number of classrooms. If local school law was actually to be enforced, then nearly 300 students would be crammed into these rooms, which would have posed a severe health and safety hazard. It was not only indoor space that was lacking. There was no outdoor recreational area to speak of- students were forced to spend recess on the rather dangerous Piccadilly Street, which was one of the main roads leading into the city. As a result, a petition was made to the School Board of Winchester for a new school building in 1924, and the road to the growth of the Douglas School made its start.

The Handley Board of Trustees was looking into facilities for white and colored children of Winchester, according to a report published in the *Winchester Evening Star* as early as December 1918. No action had been taken on the school for the colored children and in 1926 local citizens began to petition the school board for better facilities.

(July 31, 1926)

On September 5, 1927, a new milestone in the development of the Douglas School was reached upon the laying of the cornerstone of the new school on North Kent Street. Less than two months later, on November 1, the new Douglas School opened its doors for the first time.

The Kent Street building was designed by R.V. Long, a state architect. The building was constructed by Gardner and Newcome of Stephens City, Virginia. The new building contained six classrooms, a library, restrooms, and a principal's office, and had steam heat and a large outdoor play area. The building and furnishings totaled $33,217.65 and had been made possible thanks to the will of Judge John Handley, who had stipulated that he wished to have his money used for educating the poor. An article in the *Winchester Evening Star* said the school was one of the most complete colored school edifices in Virginia.

On November 1, 1927, 150 students and six teachers marched from the Old Stone Church to the new school on North Kent Street. Only grades first through ninth were offered at this time.

Winchester Evening Star

Colored School Patrons To Seek A New Building

Present Facilities and Equipment Here Are Claimed To Be Inadequate

John Mann M. E. Church was filled to the capacity last night with school patrons and tax payers of all description of the city of Winchester, who were uncompromisingly bent on improving the housing condition of their public school.

A survey on the part of a special committee headed by Prof. John H. Quiett, gave evidence that less consideration had been given the Winchester colored school regarding its seating capacity, location and playground facilities in the last few years than any town its size in the state of Virginia

School Law Neglected

The finding also revealed that in case the school law should be enforced nearly 300 children of school age would be pressed into three rooms and that three-fourths of the 183 now on roll are compelled to attend school only on half-day shift; and in addition to this congested situation the children have no ground for recreation other than the open and dangerous Piccadilly street, which is one of the main arteries leading into the city.

The building which is being used for a school house is a very old-fashioned stone structure with very inadequate ventilation and light advantages, and is far below the state requirements in sanitation.

The colored people, while having no outcry in the last ten years, are now lining up with patrons, ministers, teachers, doctors, lawyers and business men, white and colored, who are hopeful of finding a way out of the present situations.

New Building Asked

A petition from this meeting will be made through a committee to the School Board of Winchester for a new school building.

Among those pledging unstinted support to the better school are Dr. Brown, Mrs. David Anderson, Charles Lampkins, John Morris, James Robinson, I. Jackson, L. Turner, Mrs. Bettie Jackson, J. H. Quiett, S. S. Spriggs, H. C. Walker, H.A. Johnson and many others.

It was announced today that other mass meetings will be held from time to time by the colored people until they succeed in having better school facilities provided by school authorities.

Winchester Evening Star
Sat. July 31, 1926

Ground Is Broken For New Colored School Building

Plant is to be Ready for Occupancy at Beginning of Term Next Fall

Ground was broken yesterday afternoon for the erection of a school building for the colored children of Winchester, the first pick being driven into the ground by Stewart Bell, representative for the City School Board on the joint committee for the erection of the building.

In a joint meeting of the Handley Board of Trustees and the city school board, held last Tuesday night, the bid of Gardner and Newcome of $28,500 was accepted by a unanimous vote.

The actual supervision of the erection was placed under the direction of John I. Sloat of the Handley Board and Stewart Bell of the School Board.

Exterior to be Colonial

The building as proposed will present a colonial exterior and is of the one-story type, with a frontage of 90 feet and a depth of 107 feet. There will be five academic classrooms, and in addition specially built rooms for domestic science and manual training. A library is also provided, which will be operated as a branch of the Handley Library.

In order that this building might serve as a community center, the plans called for an auditorium with a fixed seating capacity of 350, which might without crowding, be increased to 400 or more. This will give the colored people of the community an assembly room of greater capacity in proportion to the colored population than is now provided for any gathering of white people.

Provision is also made for a moving picture booth, shower baths, and practically all of the modern school conveniences.

Will Rank With Best

Upon the completion of this building, Winchester will have a school house for colored children of the community which will rank for its size with any in the state, and will afford the colored children educational advantages which they have long needed.

Under the contract, the building is to be completed by September, unless there should be some unfortunate obstacle, and it is expectation of the School Board to open the session commencing 1927-28 in the new building.

The building in its construction will be under the direct supervision of Raymond V. Long, state supervisor of school buildings.

Winchester Evening Star
April 1, 1927

Cornerstone Laying Parade

Views of the parade taken on Piccadilly Street. The parade wound the streets of Winchester ending at the new Douglas School on North Kent Street for the laying of the cornerstone in 1927.

Previous Page: Douglas School band marching east on Piccadilly Street. Some person partially identified by key (Charlie Long with American flag.)

Three men on horseback lead Douglas School Cornerstone Laying Parade.
(1493-109b)

Time Line from School Board Minutes

February 18, 1924
Announced the possibility of erecting a new colored school building. A committee from the school board was to meet with the Handley Board of Trustees.

June 25, 1925
Mr. R. V. Long, a state architect was in town to discuss new building.

September 26, 1926
School Board set up special committee for new building.

November 19, 1926
The Handley Board of Trustees and the Common Council communicated to the Winchester School Board to borrow $15,000 from the State of Virginia at 3 percent interest per annum to be used for the construction of the colored school. The Handley Board of Trustees will raise the remaining $15,000 and that the building should be constructed within the $30,000 budget.

February 7, 1927
Plans and specifications for the building went to the Handley Board of Trustees and the Winchester School Board for approval.

February 14, 1927
The plans and specs were reviewed by both boards and received approval.

March 7, 1927
Bids had been received and were in excess of the $30,000 budget. Plans had to be redrawn to slightly diminish the size of the building, especially the auditorium.

March 28, 1927
The new plans and specs along with Gardner and Newcome bid which included all changes was submitted.

March 28, 1927
Joint meeting held including the Handley Board of Trustees, members of the Common Council and members of the school board met and approved the revised plans and bid.

June 3, 1927
Mr. Stewart Bell, chairman of the building committee for the colored school advised the school board that the new building was coming along nicely. A committee from Alexandria, Virginia, was visiting Winchester and upon seeing the colored school decided to erect a similar building in their city.

Masons in Douglas School Cornerstone Laying Parade. (1493-109c)

Women marching in Douglas School in Douglas School Cornerstone Laying Parade (1493-109a)

Time Line from School Board Minutes

August 3l, 1927
School Board members to meet at city hall auditorium on Labor Day 10:40 a.m. to participate in the parade to be held by the colored people for the purpose of laying the cornerstone in the new colored school.

October 17, 1927
The building is complete except for a few cabinets and

some hardware. Mr. Long, the architect, the Handley Board of Trustees and the school board to meet on October 24 for the final inspection and approval of the building.

October 24, 1927
The inspection showed there were some leaks in the roof that needed repairing and a return pipe to the

heating system which had not been installed to the architect's specifications needed to be corrected. Other than these minor corrections, the building was approved. The final cost was $33,217.65 for the building and all furnishings. The building included six classrooms, a library, restrooms and a principal's

office, as well as steam heat and a large outdoor play area. After a long anticipated wait from the announcement in 1924 until November 1, 1927, six teachers and one hundred and fifty students excitedly marched from Piccadilly Street to their brand new school on North Kent Street.

Winchester Evening Star

Cornerstone Of Douglas School Laid Yesterday

Large Outpouring of Colored People Present at Epic-Making Event In This City Yesterday.

Parade Over A Mile Long

Imposing Ceremonies Mark Efforts of White Citizens To Assist In Colored Youths Better Education.

The colored population of Winchester and widely spread territory around it had a gala day yesterday in this city when the cornerstone of the new Douglas school building on North Kent Street was laid with appropriate ceremonies, at which leading white speakers of the community paid glowing tribute to the colored people themselves and lauded the efforts of Handley Trustees and the school board of the city in rearing an imposing structure for the education of the colored youth of the city.

A parade which was nearly a mile long and in which over 1,000 people participated, preceded the cornerstone laying exercises at the school building.

There were fraternal orders from many towns and cities in the immediate vicinity of Winchester while others came from Pennsylvania, Maryland and West Virginia.

The speaker of the day was Dr. Kelly Miller, Dean of the School of Science and Art, Howard University, Washington, D.C. His address was heard by several thousand people, among them being leaders in education among the white population, who were present on the platform, or mingled in the crowd.

Dr. Miller's Speech

Dr. Miller told his people to cherish this evidence of the esteem of the white man and his willingness to assist the negro in obtaining an education. He said further that in all his experience he never witnessed more amicable relations between the races and the desire on the part of their white friends to help the colored man than this occasion afforded and he expressed the hope and belief that the two races would always dwell here in unity and peace, each mutually assisting the other

The town was filled yesterday throughout the day and far into last night by colored people, thousands of them. They were all orderly, well behaved and they represented the best of their race in this part of the country. Not a single case of disorder in the large crowd present was officially reported.

Parade Yesterday Morning

The day began with the parade at 11 o'clock yesterday morning. It was headed by a motorcycle detail from police headquarters and it passed over the principal streets which were thronged with white and colored alike.

Following the chief marshall and his aides, the parade was led by the colored Elks Band of Alexandria, Va. Behind them came official cars containing members of the Handley Trustees, the City Council, and the speakers and other participants in the exercises which were as follows:

Then came lodges of Grand United Order of Odd Fellows from Strasburg, Millwood, Front Royal, Middleburg, Va, Martinsburg, West Virginia; Masons from Winchester, Hagerstown, Maryland, and other towns; Knights of Pythias and Patriarchs from several places and visiting Elks from Hagerstown, Strasburg and Alexandria, Daughters of Elks from Strasburg and Hagerstown. The latter orders made a particularly striking and effective appearance dressed in white with purple lined capes turned backward over the shoulders, with white shoes and caps.

The second division was headed by the Douglas School Band, of this city, dressed in blue coats with white trousers. They were followed by public school pupils from Winchester, Berryville, Clarke County, Frederick County and a number of other places. The girls were attired in white frocks with white caps. Also in this division were other visiting lodges of Masons, Pythians, Household of Ruth, the Sunday schools from this and other places and community clubs.

The third division was headed by the Charles Town, (West Virginia) band and was followed by Household of Ruth Lodge, Grand Order of Odd Fellows of Winchester

The parade was the largest of colored people ever seen here and it has been declared to have been an imposing spectacle. Visualizing, as it did, the steady progress upward of the colored race in the community.

After passing over the principal streets, the parade was disbanded at the new school building, where the cornerstone exercises were held beginning at two o'clock.

In the absence of Edward B. Morris of Chicago, grand master of the United Order of Odd Fellows of the United States, who was to have officiated, the cornerstone was laid by John Wanzer, of Middleburg, assisted by the Odd Fellows.

Continued next page

County Schools

The following schools served colored children for grades one through seven. Children wishing for more educationattended Douglas School in Winchester.

Continued from previous page

Supt. Duffey - Introduces Speakers

Supt. H.S. Duffey, of the Handley Schools of Winchester, introduced the speakers who were, in addition to Dr. Kelly Miller, of Howard University, President R. Gray Williams, of the Handley Board of Trustees, and President John M. Steck, of the Winchester School Board, and A.T. Shirley District Grand Secretary of the Odd Fellows of Virginia.

The arrangements for the cornerstone laying were under the charge of Powell W. Gibson, principal of the Douglas School, chairman, and J.M. Morris, J.F. Robinson, L.H. Nickens, James Wells, and Charles Lampkins, the latter being treasurer. Lloyd P. Fisher was grand marshall and James Wells and Edward Doakes were assistants.

Last night the Elks' Band of Alexandria gave a concert at City Hall Auditorium while an orchestra concert was given at Evans Hotel where refreshments were served.

The new school building, where the cornerstone was laid yesterday, is a part of the John Handley School system and was made possible through the will of Judge John Handley. It is now being completed at a cost of over $30,000 and is one of the most complete colored public school edifices in Virginia.

Winchester Evening Star
September 6, 1927

Middletown Colored School, Frederick County, Virginia, 1934. The school was closed in 1960. (199-12)

Cedar Hill Colored School and outbuildings, Frederick County, 1934. The building was destroyed by a fire in 2006. (199-35)

The partnership between the Winchester School Board and the Frederick County School system began in 1934. Mr. Leslie Kline of Frederick County inquired of the Winchester School Board if a small group of negro students from Opequon and Stephens City could attend Douglas School. It was moved and seconded by the Winchester School Board that these students be allowed to attend Douglas providing the number of students did not cause overcrowding conditions in the different departments of Douglas. The first tuition was set at $40.00 per student per year and by the early 1960s had grown to $350.00 per student per year.

Leetown Colored School, Frederick County, Virginia, 1934. Unidentified child on steps It closed in 1940. (199-7)

Stephens City Colored School, Frederick County, Virginia, 1934. Unidentified students in front. The school was closed in 1960. (199-31)

Colored (black) school in Strasburg, Virginia.The Section on the left of photo was the original building.
1493-18a

Graduation Day at Stephens City Colored School, c. 1950. Shirley Shields, Frances Washington, Eleanore Finley Burks (teacher), _____ Stern, Lula Medley

Douglas School Branch Library

This branch in the school building for colored residents has not been as active as desired, largely due to the lack of suitable elementary books to fit the needs of those of our colored population who have leisure time for reading. It is hoped this deplorable condition may be remedied during the coming year, at least to some extent.

The branch was open 166 days in 1935 and a total of 399 books were borrowed for home use. It goes without saying that the books available were used much more for reference work during school hours.

Winchester Evening Star
January 14, 1936

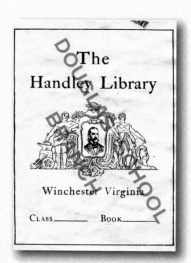

The Douglas Beacon May 1939

Editorial Staff
Sadie Jackson   Fannie Weaver   Elenora Langford
John Poulson   Roland Harper

Due to the fact that the school board is adding one more year of work next term, namely the tenth grade, our principal announces that there will not be commencement exercises this spring. However we do have some very interesting events coming off during June week.

The school exhibit which includes the Home Economics and Manual Training will begin on Wednesday June 7th; on Friday afternoon at 1:30 there will be held on the school athletic field, a field day exercise. There will be races, broad jumps, high jumps, and many other interesting events for both boys and girls.

On Friday evening at 8:30 June 9th, our closing day program will be given. This program will consist of boys and girls from each grade in the entire school. Don't forget the dates for our big June week. Come and meet your friends here, you'll not regret it.

appreciated by all those attending now, and those who have graduated in previous years. There are some perhaps who will return to continue schooling, if the course is extended. If true, the class to enter next year will be considerably larger.

Some of these things to help make this course a success are, first, for the student and the parents to acquire a cooperative attitude toward the teachers, second, for the students to get into the attitude of study and not play, and third, for the students to appreciate the way in which the lessons are taught. If the students acquire the attitude of study, and work with the Teachers and all who are trying to help, it will be as good as any school of the same standard. An idea, "Of more work and less play", will be a great help to the success of the school. If these and many other important things be practiced by the student body, we will have an Alma Mater we all will be proud of.

By Elenora Langford

EDITORAL

Prospects of a High – School in Winchester

There are prospects of a Senior High School for the students of Douglass. A Senior High has been wanted for a long time. We are hoping that it will be a success. It will be

School Board Acts on Expansions and Additions

The question of higher education was discussed at the school board late in 1938. They decided not to raise the issue at this time. The board also asked the school superintendent to inquire as to the cost of sending a class to the regional school in Manassas, Virginia. This question was raised again in early 1939. The board decided to make permanent arrangements including adding another grade to Douglas next year and another grade the following year. In September of 1939 the offerings at Douglas were extended to the tenth grade. A portion of the basement was converted to a class room and one additional teacher was hired to take care of the extra instruction.

In July 1940, the board resolved to add two rooms to Douglas and to hire one additional teacher to increase the offerings at Douglas. John W. Rosenberger submitted the lowest bid of $4,443.65. The two rooms were completed and presented by the Handley Board of Trustees to the Winchester School Board in December 1940. The offerings at Douglas were extended to the eleventh grade beginning with the 1941 school year.

In 1945, a committee of five local colored citizens petitioned the school board asking for certain needs at the Douglas School. The list included a room for domestic science, vocational training, a gymnasium, baseball grounds, a band, and a truant office. The board agreed to have the educational committee make an inspection of Douglas relating to the issues raised by the five local patrons.In November 1948, the Superintendent of Winchester Schools met with the State Superintendent and Assistant Superintendent of Public Education and the Superintendents of surrounding counties to discuss plans for a regional high school for Negro students. A request was made by Warren County to have their high school students attend Douglas. Winchester's Board voted to honor this agreement and admit pupils from Warren County providing the number requested would not be increased and the Winchester School Board reserves the right to terminate the agreement if necessary. Mr. Aylor, Superintendent of Frederick County, requested permission for 7th grade students from Frederick County to be allowed to attend Douglas. This request was rejected by Winchester because it would cause overcrowding at Douglas. High School students from Woodstock, Strasburg, and Frederick County rode buses into Winchester each day for classes. The buses were always old, no longer used for white students and often had no heat. Often a male high school student was responsible for driving the bus of fellow high school students getting them to school on time and safe.

Five years passed before any action was taken. Minutes from the March 20, 1950 school board meeting read, "Since our last communication to the council, the board has come to the conclusion that we must also expend a considerable sum for an addition to the colored school. This expenditure is in our judgment necessary, not because of any increase in enrollment, as is the case in the white school, but in order to avoid court action which might be brought at any time on the part of the colored population claiming discrimination. While we are providing for our Negro pupils better facilities and offerings than are provided in most school divisions, we are not providing everything offered in the white school. For instance, there is no provision for physical education: our shop and science offering is limited: our library facilities are not adequate. We do not provide for commercial subjects. If these additions in offerings are to be made more space is necessary. Therefore the board will add this to the list of building additions required."

In 1963, the final expansion was a new home economics room, a science lab, a music room, and one more classroom. In 1966 Winchester integrated its school system and Douglas School was closed.

Douglas School brings to mind many cherished memories. We can all recall the closeness of the faculty and students. We can remember the many football and basketball championships. We also recall the many times the glee club or band went to a music festival and came home with a superior rating. There are many who went beyond Douglas and obtained their bachelor, masters, or doctorate degrees. Whatever memory, great or small, Douglas started in a humble three-room school that earlier settlers had built as a church.

Douglas School
Addition (555-157)

DOUGLAS SCHOOL NEWS

The faculty and students of the Douglas High School are sorry to relate that they do not have an Industrial Arts teacher this term, but are very much pleased to have biology added to the course, taught by Miss McKinney.

Mrs. Wright, who has formerly taught first grade, is now teaching the seventh, and Miss Estelle Mitchell has charge of the class formerly taught by Mrs. Wright.

There are 200 students thus far, and a number of them come from Strasburg, Stephens City, Front Royal, Leetown, and Clearbrook.

Three of the five students who graduated last June have entered college. Weaver Banks and John Poulson entered Virginia State College in Petersburg, and Roland Harper entered Storer College, Harpers Ferry, W. Va.

Winchester Evening Star
September 18, 1943

Dedication Tonight Of Douglas Addition

Dedicatory ceremonies for the new $150,000 addition to the Douglas Colored School will be held in the school auditorium at 8:15 o'clock tonight, with Dr. A. G. Richardson, associate superintendent of elementary and secondary schools of the State Department of Education, Richmond, as the principal speaker.

Announcement of the program was made this morning by Superintendent Garland R. Quarles, of the Winchester City Schools. Mr. Quarles said that the Douglas Glee Club, under the direction of Mrs. Laura B. Turner, will sing.

John H. Rosenberger, chairman of the City Board of Education, will make the presentation of the structure on behalf of the board, and it will be accepted for the faculty by Kirk N. Gaskins, principal. Acceptance on behalf of the students will be Miss Joan Eliott, a member of the senior class.

The invocation will be by the Rev. Julius S. Carroll, pastor of John Mann Methodist Church, and the benediction will be by the Rev. Chester M. Comer, of Mt. Carmel Baptist Church.

The brick addition, which was started last April under the supervision of Shockey and Sons, general contractors, was completed in December and moved into during the Christmas school holidays. It includes three classrooms, a library, gymnasiums for both boys and girls, a physical education room, shop, and kitchen.

Winchester Star, 1952

Twenty-two members of Douglas High School faculty and surrounding county faculty, taking a required extension course in Mr. Jackson's classroom at Douglas School. The date of the photo was April 11, 1947. Some persons identified are Alma Louada Layton, Francis M. Jackson, Hattie M. Lea, Margaree Washington, Effie McKinney, Lovelena Lomax Marcus, Anna Quiett Brooks Tokes, Blanche Gibson Moten, Kirk Nathaniel Gaskins Sr. (principal), Marcia Taper. (1493-54)

Faculty and Staff

Principals

R. Page Hall, principal 1875–1908

Mr. Hall was born in Virginia (now West Virginia) in October 1857. The earliest evidence of Hall in Winchester, Virginia, is from a document taken from an old Douglas

John Mann Methodist Church Parsonage, 114 East Piccadilly Street, Winchester, Virginia. Mrs. Bell Hall and Mr. Page Hall on the front porch of their home. (1493-53a)

High School staff yearbook, claiming that Hall was principal as early as 1875. However, the first students did not arrive at the school until 1878, which means that Hall could very well have been involved with administrative work and the preparation necessary for establishing the school and designing its curriculum.

According to the Shenandoah Valley Rail Road Directory of 1878-1879, Hall had two separate jobs. This was common for area teachers, as the pay would not have been a living wage. Hall was listed as a grocer on the west end of Piccadilly Street in 1878, the same year students began going to the school. In the same directory, it lists Hall as living on Cecil Street, east of Braddock Street, some blocks away from the Old Stone Presbyterian Church.

Hall was married, at the age of 30, to Laura L. B. Hall in 1887. They had three children, though only two were living in 1900. According to the Winchester Directory of 1898–1899, Hall lived in a house located at 119 West Monmouth Street, along with his wife and their two daughters, Mary and Alice. The 1900 Census of Winchester, Ward 2, indicates that along with his immediate family, his sister-in-law, Hattie E. Turner, and his niece, Edna Turner, also lived with the family.

His two daughters were born in Winchester while he was principal at the Winchester Colored School. Mary, the oldest, was born in January of 1888 and Alice was born two years later in 1890. By the time of his daughters' births, Hall was no longer working as a grocer, but instead as a barber according to the Winchester Directory of 1898-1899.

Hall retired as the principal of the Winchester Colored School in 1908 at the age of 51. By the end of his administration as principal, the total population of Winchester was 6,739 persons, 1,760 of which were listed as colored in the 1905 Winchester Directory. Little is known of Hall after 1908.

Rev. John H. Quiett, principal 1908–1915

He was born on December 25, 1859, in Warrenton, Virginia, just prior to the Civil War, an event that had a dramatic effect on his life. His father was absent for the entirety of his life, having fled to Canada the year that John was born, and he lost all contact with his mother after the Confederate army raided Manassas during the Second Battle of Bull Run. Like many lost children during the Civil War in Virginia, Quiett made his way to Alexandria, Virginia.

Quiett attended school there until he was 17 years old. He then attended the Hampton Institute, which was not a public school, and because of the absence of his parents, John had to find a way to pay for his schooling. He was able to attend school, in part with assistance from a Catholic organization in Richmond, which helped pay his way and provided an additional fifty cents allowance. This was not the only source of income John had while attending Hampton Institute, though. General Samuel Chapman Armstrong, the director of the school, also lent Quiett a knitting machine, with which he knitted his way through school. His time at Hampton Institute ended with his graduation in 1880 in a class that

included Booker T. Washington. Quiett had an extensive history with school systems in Virginia. He first worked in a school in Manassas, Virginia, and also helped in the creation of another school in Woodlawn, Virginia. He worked at these schools for eighteen years before making his way to Winchester. Quiett first worked in Winchester under the

direction of Rev. Burrell at the Mount Carmel Freewill Baptist Church. Quiett only stayed one year. He became principal of the Winchester Colored School in 1908, after the retirement of R. Page Hall. He was principal for seven years, retiring in 1915 from the position.

Rev. Quiett married Gertrude A. Moss of Loudoun County, Virginia and they had five children. In 1934, John Quiett passed away followed by Mrs. Quiett in 1947. Both are buried in Orrick Cemetery, Winchester, Virginia.

John Henry Quiett, principal of Old Stone School. date unknown. This school was later to become known as Douglas School from 1916 to 1927 until the new Douglas School building was opened. (599-32)

Powell W. Gibson, Principal
1916–1940

Powell Gibson was probably Douglas School's most influential leader. Gibson was born in Middleburg, Virginia, on April 16, 1875, the son of Mr. and Mrs. Edward Gibson. He first completed elementary school in

A portrait of Powell W. Gibson, who served as Douglas School's principal for twenty-five years. (204-66)

Middleburg; however, like the school he would eventually become principal of, it did not offer anything past the grade school level. So, like many other students who wished to continue their education, Powell had to move to Washington, D.C., in

hopes of graduating from high school. He attended Wayland Seminary School, and went on to study at a number of universities. He graduated from Maryland State Normal School, though he also attended Carnegie College, Virginia Union University, and the University of Pennsylvania.

Powell Gibson, according to one of his published essays, developed a distinct teaching philosophy while studying at the various upper level schools in the United States. He believed that special training for teachers helped shorten the period of "necessarily amateurish practice to eliminate some of the earlier errors and to augment the successful efforts." He mentioned in the same essay that he liked the notion of developing teaching styles from personal experience at the head of the classroom; however, he did not think this particular style of learning was efficient. He believed that it is equally, if not more so, important to learn from the previous teachers in order to better understand how to run a classroom efficiently and successfully.

He also stressed the importance of common sense when teaching . He had three reasons for making this statement. First, common sense allows for any teacher in a rural area to adjust to the lifestyle of the rural community. Second, he believed common sense was the best way a rural teacher could affiliate with the rural community. Third, common sense is the most important tool necessary to take students as they are, and lead them to the "higher plane," the goal of education. Gibson constantly stressed the importance of raising the community in order to raise an individual. He was quoted as saying that rural teachers needed to "get under the burden in order to shoulder it." He understood that rural teachers were not paid well, but he disregarded this burden by saying that progress continued to be made during his time as a principal, and that teachers were not only financially paid, but also had the most satisfactory payment of teaching: the progress of the students themselves. Before arriving as the principal of the Winchester Colored School, Gibson was principal of Brown School in Manassas, Virginia, for eight years, and also served as the supervisor of the colored schools in Chestertown and Kent County, Maryland, for three years. He moved to Winchester in 1915 after the retirement of Rev. J. H. Quiett, where he would take over as principal of the Winchester Colored School.

Gibson served as the principal of the school from 1915 through 1940, an impressive 25 years. The first, and arguably one of the biggest contributions to the school, was changing the name. Prior to the arrival of Gibson, the school was simply known as the Winchester Colored School, or the Old Stone Church School for Coloreds. Gibson, in order to honor one of the most famed African-Americans in United States History, declared the school to be named Douglas High School, in honor of Frederick Douglass.

This was not Gibson's only contribution to the school. By the mid-1920s, the Old Stone Presbyterian Church in which the school met was no longer an adequate building to house the students; on their quest for higher education.

According to the *Winchester Evening Star* in 1924, the church where the students met was "filled to its capacity last night with school patrons and tax-payers of all description of the city of Winchester, who were uncompromisingly bent on improving the housing condition of their public school." There were around 300 students in attendance at the school in the mid-1920s. The building in which they met had three rooms, with poor air circulation and lighting. It also mentioned that the state requirements for sanitation were not even close to being met. There were so many students that they could not even meet on a full day schedule, and so students only met in half day increments.

Gibson retired as principal of Douglas High School in 1940, having provided more than forty-five years of educational service to the surrounding community. After retirement as principal, he continued to work as a substitute teacher for Frederick County and Winchester City Public Schools. He was also the author of a book of poems entitled *Grave and Comic Rhyme*, which included a poem dedicated to Frederick Douglass. He also authored two plays: *Jake Among the Indians*, and *The King of the Mandingoes*.

When Gibson first arrived in the city of Winchester in 1915, he bought a house east of town. The house was rundown and badly in need of repair. However, Gibson was known for saying "take what you have, and make it what you want", a testament both to his character and his teaching philosophy. Powell lived in the home with his wife, Hattie B. Gibson.

They had two children, a daughter, Blanche, and a son, Powell Willard Jr.

Gibson died on May 3, 1959, after attending one last church service at Shiloh Baptist Church in Middleburg. It is said that he died peacefully, yet unexpectedly, in his swing in his front yard. According to the death notice in the *Winchester Evening Star* on May 4, 1959: "Powell W. Gibson, at the age of 84, of 19 East Street, died suddenly yesterday morning at his home after attending church service." It lists his survivors as his wife Hattie, his daughter Blanche Moten, his son Willard, and his granddaughter, Loretta Moten, all living in Winchester, and a sister, Gertrude Grimes of Philadelphia, Pennsylvania.

The funeral service was held on Wednesday, May 6, 1959, at Mount Carmel Baptist Church. Pastor Rev. Melford W. Walker, assisted by Rev. R.R. Robinson, conducted the service. Professor Gibson was buried at Solon Cemetery in his hometown of Middleburg, Virginia.

Kirk N. Gaskins, Sr.
1940-1966

Kirk N. Gaskins Sr. became the new principal of the Douglas High School following the 25-year administration of Powell Gibson, Gaskins had taught at the school the previous three years.

Kirk Gaskins was a Winchester native, born in 1903 to Andrew and Emma Kirk Gaskins, and raised on South Loudoun Street. Gaskins always had strong ties to the Douglas High School, having been a student

when the school was located at the Old Stone Church on 310 East Piccadilly Street. He graduated from Douglas School in 1918. However, at the time the school only offered a program for grades one through nine, so like many other Douglas School alumni, he had to complete his high

Kirk N. Gaskins Sr., Principal of Douglas High School, 1940 (1493-9)

school education outside the city of Winchester. He completed high school and junior college at Storer College in Harpers Ferry, West Virginia. He then went to Virginia Union University in Richmond, Virginia. At Virginia Union University, he graduated with a Bachelor of Arts degree. He studied and majored in algebra, which he later taught, and received a minor in Latin.

Prior to coming to Douglas in 1937, Gaskins served as principal at Andrew Jackson School in Luray, Virginia, for five years. During Gaskins' administration at Douglas High School there were a number of changes to both the programs offered and the building itself. In 1940, two new classrooms were added to the school, and the following year the school extended its educational program to include grades ten and eleven. Twelve years later, in 1952 the school underwent another expansion, when four new classrooms, a new library, an industrial arts shop, a gymnasium, and a cafeteria. In 1953, a full school curriculum of twelve grades was offered. He also oversaw another transformation in 1962 when a new home economics room, a science lab, a music room, and an additional classroom were added. Gaskins became the administrative assistant to Jacob L. Johnson, the superintendent of John Handley High School, in 1966 when Winchester city schools were integrated. He retired in 1968.

On Monday, January 26, 1981, Kirk N. Gaskins died at the Winchester Memorial Hospital after a short illness. *The Winchester Evening Star* dedicated an article to the former principal of Douglas High School in the January 29, 1981, edition. His funeral was held at Mount Carmel Baptist Church on January 30, 1981, and he was buried in Orrick Cemetery in Winchester. Rev. John G. Scott presided.

Jacob Johnson is quoted in the *Star*, saying: "I always found him very cooperative and was always interested in the welfare of the total school system. He did his job competently and was always a very friendly person to work with."

Gaskins was a Mason, a member of the American Association of Retired Persons, as well as a member of the NAACP, according to the same article. He was also a member of the Virginia State Teachers Association during his long career as an educator in the Shenandoah Valley and surrounding area.

His surviving family members were his widow, Ella Finley Gaskins; two daughters, Joy G. Jordan and June G. Davis; three sons, Kirk N. Gaskins Jr., Andrew T. Gaskins, and Beverly P. Gaskins; a sister, Nannie G. Mitchell; and nine grandchildren and two nieces.

Principals Remember

The autos that pass my humble home sometimes get out of control and play havoc with fences while the B&O trains, to date, have kept steadily to the track.

In compliance with the request to say something about the local Douglas School, it was thought prudent to submit my hastily prepared remarks to manuscript in order to keep somewhere near "to the track."

Through the legacy of Judge Handley and the consideration of the local school officials, the Colored people of Winchester have on North Kent Street a school building that compares favorably (if indeed it does not form a contrast) with that of any community of like size in the state. After a great deal of care and pains over a space of ten years the lawn fronting the building now presents a pleasing view in season, through attention of the janitor and the larger boys. The rectangular pillars at the entrance to the grounds were made within a few hours by the boys from waste lumber and painted white to conform agreeably with the stately colonnade adorning the building. There is a spacious auditorium with a seating capacity of 400, a special library room with more than 3,000 volumes to which others are added from time to time. Six teachers are regularly employed, covering a course of nine years, or through junior high school. When the pamphlets relative to the Handley Fund were distributed in 1918 it was planned upon the completion of the new school building to carry the children through junior high school to meet the needs of the ten or twelve who would complete the course. Forthwith, however, permission was obtained to include this work immediately, with the outcome that of the first class of ten, eight finished senior high school elsewhere and five finished college.

The school has a very promising glee club, a male quartet and a school band, the latter under direction of a teacher from Storer College. (Storer College was located in Harpers Ferry, West Virginia)

In the manual training department the boys are doing excellent woodwork which is very valuable training, whatever their future employment may be. It would certainly be well if some, at least, could make it their life work.

In the domestic science department the girls are given careful training in cooking and sewing and very creditable demonstrations are made from time to time. It would be well if fine cooking could be classified among the seven fine arts.

Playground equipment was given the children several years ago and a director is employed for the summer months. Much of the remaining portion of the twelve acre plot could be profitably used for gardening under a trained Smith Hughes agent. There is a constant agitation for this blessing and it is believed it will be secured in the near future.

Finally, it is a grim struggle day after day to triumph over the counteracting evil forces that beset the children's pathway—to get them to cherish what is right and abhor what is wrong—to become worthwhile, thrifty, law-abiding citizens—this is the problem we are earnestly striving to solve.

Powell Gibson, c. 1937

Principals Remember

As I close my career I am proud of many things:

First, I am completing thirty years of service in the Winchester School System. I have missed only ten days during that time for illness.

Second, I was born and reared in this cty and had the opportunity to serve as teacher and principal in my home town school.

My third reason I shall never forget. When I became principal, a well-known educator of this city gave me this advice.

I want you to run this school, do a good job, but don't do anything crazy. I remembered this down through the years. So tonight I can say with pride to you and to him, that, I ran the school, I did a good job, and I didn't do anything crazy.

I should like to express my appreciation to the Winchester School Board for its support and kind consideration through the years. I also want to thank you for your cooperation and support.

I also want to express my appreciation to my devoted wife for her patience in putting up with me all these years. Now last, but by no means least, I want to extend my appreciation to Mr. Johnson, whom I have found to be a fine gentleman and a pleasure to work with.

Now to you who are still in the field, I say rededicate yourselves to the unfinished task. The work of the world is not completed yet. A better way must be found and established to maintain world peace. More communication with dialogue must be set up. Outer space and all of its mysterious ramifications including reaching the moon must be conquered. These goals must be met by the youngsters in your classrooms with your guidance and instruction only.

I wish you good health, happiness, a long life, and God's blessings.

K. N. Gaskins, June 3, 1968

Faculty and Staff

Over the years, Douglas was blessed with an abundance of excellent teachers who strived to help their students become "the best they could be." Records, letters, and reports show that our teachers attended summer school and state teacher associations to keep up with new ideas and strategies to help the students of Douglas that they not only taught but cherished. Most of this information is taken from articles published in the *Winchester* *Evening Star* these reports were written by Douglas students.

There are some student records in the Archives at the Handley Library that shows the teaching staff from 1900 through 1908 were: John H. Quiett, Miss Lena Webb, and Miss Isabella Strange. The class size for these teachers was as low as 36 and as high as 70 students per teacher.

1927-1928

First teachers at new Douglas School, 1927-1928. Front row, left to right row: Hattie Mitchell, Lovelena Lomax, Anna Quiett Brooks; 2nd row: William Marcus, Prof. Powell W. Gibson, Principal. (204-6)

1936-1937

Douglas School Faculty, school year 1936-1937. Front row, left to right: Marie B. Briscoe, Hattie M. Lea, Lovelena Lomax, Anna Brooks Tokes; back row Taylor Floyd Finley, Powell W. Gibson (Principal). (618-30)

1938-1940

Douglas School Faculty, c. 1938-1940. Front row, left to right: Kirk N. Gaskins Sr., Powell W. Gibson (principal), Simon Cook; back row: Anna Q. Brooks Tokes, Lovelena Lomax Marcus, Blanche Gibson Moten, Nerissa Wright, Hattie M. Lea. (618-24)

1944-1945

Douglas School teachers sitting at school front entrance; date estimated as 1945. Seated, left to right: Anna Brooks Tokes, Francis M. Jackson, Hattie M. Lea, Kirk N. Gaskins Sr. (Principal), Nerissa Wright, Clarence Davis; standing: Effie McKinney, Lovelena Lomax Marcus, Blanche Gibson Moten, Alma Louada Layton.
(618-22)

1950-1951

Douglas High School faculty in front of school building for the school year 1950-1951. Seated, left to right: Blanche Gibson Moten, Otelia A. Pegram, Kirk N. Gaskins Sr., Effie McKinney, Margaree Washington; standing, left to right: Anna Q. Brooks Tokes, Francis Jackson, Lovelena Lomax Marcus, Edwin Barksdale, Mattie Russell, Charles Dendy, Alma Louada Layton.
(203-7)

Winchester Evening Star

Mr. Thomas Haywood was introduced as a member of the Douglas Faculty who will have charge of manual training. He was a recent graduate of Hampton and during the summer took a course in aviation. Douglas teachers were well represented in summer school. Mrs. Lea attended Howard University, Mrs. Tokes and Mrs. Moten attended Storer College, Mrs. Wright and Miss Lomax attended Virginia State. Mr. Jackson received his B.S. Degree from Hampton Institute at the summer convocation and did graduate work toward his master's degree.

Winchester Evening Star
September 26, 1941

The District 7 Teachers Association had their annual meeting at Douglas on Saturday, November 14, at Douglas School. Among their focus was the 7 Point War Program for Schools in Virginia. Garland Quarles, superintendent of Winchester School System, gave the main address and stressed that it was the teacher's job to train their students to adjust to wartime conditions. Kirk N. Gaskins was elected vice president of the association for the coming year.

Winchester Evening Star
November 23, 1942

Mr. Griffin, the Industrial Arts Teacher, has been drafted. Mr. Powell Gibson, the former principal, is substituting in his place.

Winchester Evening Star
December 7, 1942

Mrs. Nerissa T. Wright won a prize in The Education Post Office Contest sponsored by the Afro-American newspaper of Baltimore. The industrial arts teacher was listed as Mr. Edwin Wesley.

Winchester Evening Star
May 8, 1943

The faculty and students were sorry that they had no industrial arts teacher for this term. Biology was added to the course work and was being taught by Miss McKinney. Mrs. Wright was moved to teach the 7th grade and Miss Estelle Mitchell is now teaching the 1st grade.

Winchester Evening Star
September 18, 1943

The Douglas School Staff has contributed 100 percent to the war fund drive of the American Red Cross.

Winchester Evening Star
March 3, 1944

One of our former teachers, Mr. Haywood, with his youngest brother and wife spent the weekend in the city.

Winchester Evening Star
September 15, 1945

One of our former teachers, Mr. Simon Cook and his wife visited the city of Winchester and Douglas School last week. Mr. Cook has recently been discharged from the U.S. Navy. Everyone was pleased to see him.

Winchester Evening Star
May 10, 1946

F. M. Jackson and Miss Alma Louada Layton, members of the Douglas School faculty will attend the 62nd annual convention of the Virginia Teachers Association opening Wednesday at Virginia Union University.

Winchester Evening Star
October 27, 1949

March 19, 1948 – Miss Effie McKinney has been nominated for consideration in the "Best Teacher" contest. She has received a certificate of honor for doing a fine job of teaching. Douglas congratulates her and hopes sincerely that she will be awarded one of the final grand prizes at the end of their school year. Other teachers receiving honor certificates are Mrs. Anna Tokes, Mrs. Lovelena Marcus, Mrs. Margaree Washington and Mr. Francis Jackson.

Winchester Evening Star
March 19, 1948

Douglas School classroom, c. 1950. Henry Battle's class at Douglas School. Persons identified (left to right) as (first row seats) Faye Long; (standing) Henry Battle (teacher); (second row of seats) Kenneth Willis, Closia Gene King, Mary Brown; (third row of seats) John Alsberry, Joseph Shields, Herman Jackson III, Phylis Veney; (last rows of seats) Leroy Woodson, Charles Finley, Paul Williams, Lucien Bannister, George Anthony, and Donna Dixon. (1710-9)

Winchester Evening Star

At a recent meeting, Charles Dendy, who has been very active in coaching the Bulldogs, was appointed vice president of the Tri State Athletic Union. Last year Coach Dendy's Bulldogs won 2nd place in football.

Winchester Evening Star
October 3, 1950

The four teachers who left Tuesday to attend the Virginia State Teacher's Meeting in Richmond have returned. The teachers are: Effie M. McKinney, Edwin Barksdale, Alma Layton and Francis M. Jackson.

Winchester Evening Star
November 6, 1950

The Douglas faculty and student body extend their sympathy to the families of the late Mrs. Helen V. Parks and the late Miss Lizzie Thompson. Miss Thompson was a retired teacher of the Winchester school system.

Winchester Evening Star
February 16, 1952

All Winchester schools will be closed on Friday so that the faculty members can attend the annual meeting of the District G section of the Virginia Education Association. Negro school faculties will meet at the same time in Waynesboro.

Winchester Evening Star
October 7, 1952

The annual meeting of the Seventh District Teachers Association will be held at Douglas School, Friday. Classes will not be held. Mrs. J. Rupert Picott, Executive Secretary of the Virginia Teacher's Association and Mrs. Margaret T. Haley, assistant supervisor of elementary education in the State Department of Education, will be the guest speakers. Divisions comprising the Seventh District are: Harrisonburg, Staunton, Waynesboro, Winchester, Augusta, Frederick, Clarke, Page, Highland, Rockingham and Shenandoah counties.

Winchester Evening Star
October 7, 1952

The faculty is attending the District Teachers Association meeting in Harrisonburg Friday at Lucy Simms High School.

Winchester Evening Star
October 4, 1957

Douglas children will have Friday off while the faculty there is host to District 7 Virginia Teacher's Association which meets here this year.

Winchester Evening Star
October 2, 1958

The teachers of Douglas School will be among those attending the District 7 teacher's meeting at the West Luray School on Saturday. Dr. W. H. Robinson, director, division of education Hampton Institute, and the Rev. Melford Walker of Douglas School, acting president of the district, will preside.

Winchester Evening Star
October 2, 1959

1951-1952
Douglas High School faculty, sitting outside school. Date given is 1952. Front row, left to right, seated: Effie McKinney, Blanche Gibson Moten, Kirk N. Gaskins, Sr (principal)., Margaree Washington, Alma Louada Layton; second row, left to right: Francis M. Jackson, Anna Q. Brooks Tokes, Lovelena Lomax Marcus, Mattie Russell, Norris Hite, Irene Wallace, Mildred E. Leigh, Charles Dendy. (1493-55)

1958-1959
Douglas School Faculty, school year uncertain possibly 1960. Front row, left to right: Blanche Gibson Moten, Mattie Russell Cross, Effie McKinney Davis, Kirk N. Gaskins Sr. (principal), Margaree Washington, Dorothy Moorman, Hester Harris; Second row, left to right: Tuscan Jasper, Margaret Williams, Lovelena Lomax Marcus, Francis M. Jackson, Ruth Barksdale, Dorothy Dandridge, Henry Moss Brooks. (618-33)

1963-1964

Douglas High School faculty and staff for the school year 1963-64. Front row, left to right, seated: Henry Moss Brooks, Edwin K. Barksdale, Margaree Washington, Kirk N. Gaskins Sr. (principal), Emma Singletary, Inez Mercer, Tuscan Jasper, Henry M. Battle; second row, left to right: Hester Harris, Lovelena Lomax Marcus, Mattie Russell Cross, Blanche Gibson Moten, Mary L. Byrd, Effie McKinney Davis, Gladys Vinson, Iona Robinson, Shirley Bruton, Edna Jasper, Rosa B. Francis. Ethel W. Wheeler was also on faculty/staff but is not in this picture. (1493-57)

1964-1965

Faculty for the last graduating class of Douglas School, 1965-1966. Front row left to right: Blanche Gibson Moten, Hester Harris, Kirk N. Gaskins Sr. (principal), Inez Mercer, Barbara Williams; second row, standing: Mattie R. Cross, Edwin K. Barksdale, Elizabeth Ashford, Shirley Bruton, Iona Robinson, Henry M. Brooks, Effie McKinney Davis, Lovelena Lomax Marcus, Roumaine Lett, Margaree Washington, Henry Battle, Gloria Davis. (1493-26)

1965-1966

Douglas School faculty and staff, 1966. Front row, left to right: Blanche Gibson Moten, Mary L. Byrd, Shirley Bruton, Kirk N. Gaskins Sr., Margaree Washington, Gladys S. Vinson, Barbara Williams; second row, left to right: unidentified, (head almost completely cut off,) Elizabeth Ashford, Hester Harris, Mattie R. Cross, Edwin K. Barksdale, Henry M. Brooks, Effie M. Davis, Inez Mercer, Glen L. Gore, Ethel W. Wheeler, Iona Robinson, Lovelena Lomax Marcus. (1493-58)

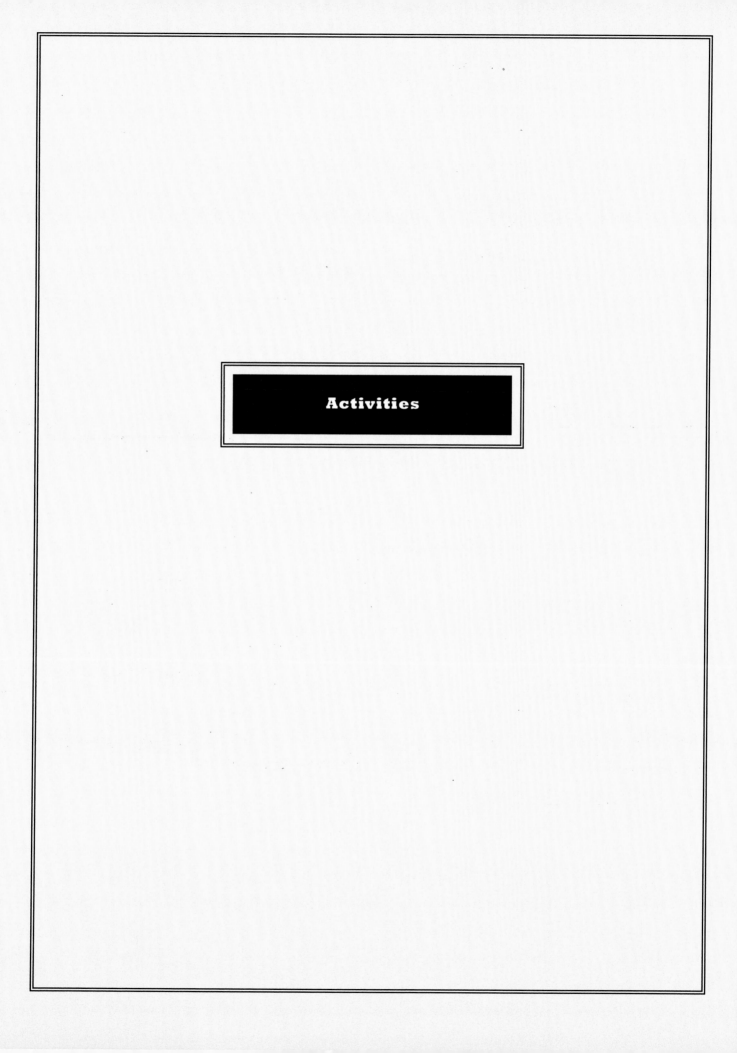

Activities

Student, Community, and Recreational Activities

The Douglas building was the pride of the local community and was often used by churches and civic organizations. The back portion of the Douglas lot was used as a playground for the black youth of Winchester.

Douglas was a hub for student activities that allowed students to discover and fine tune their talents. Assembly programs were held each Friday and each class was assigned a week where they were responsible for the program. Each class had to also attend the weekly assembly. Plays and Declamation Contests were sometimes held in the evenings so that parents and patrons could attend.

This chapter will give you some insight into student community and playground activities.

Douglas School marching unit in parade c. 1960. Left to right: Virginia Walker (supporting right side of banner), unknown, Harriet Washington (in all white), unknown, unknown, Jacqueline Williams, Mary Frances Washington, Ellen Delores Dyer (in dark skirts), Sharon Walker with glockenspiel. (555-102 thl)

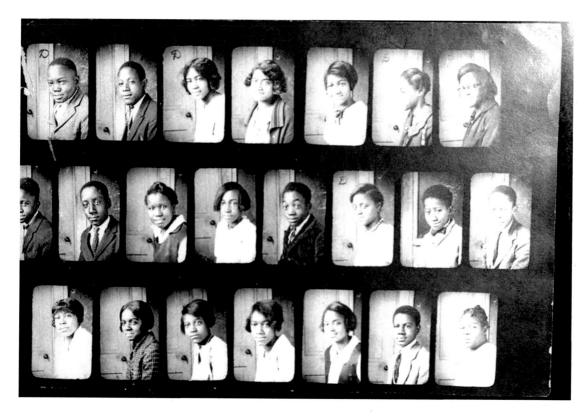

1927-1928 composite photograph of twenty-two Douglas School students. Top row, left to right: John Washington, Cornelius Conley, Mirara Conley, Beatrice Lee Finley, Josephine Jackson, unidentified, unidentified, Gray; middle row, left to right, unidentified, Phil Washington, Katherine Shelton, Lilly Wilkerson, unidentified, unidentified, Leonard Greene, unidentified; bottom row, left to right: unidentified, Rosie Bartlett, unidentified, unidentified, unidentified, unidentified, unidentified. (204-7 thl)

Powell W. Gibson (top right) and fourteen Douglas School students, c. 1930. Top row, left to right: Famie Weaver, Germain Ford, Anne Elizabeth Brooks, Carl Greene, Powell Gibson; middle row, left to right: John Triplett , unidentified, unidentified, Lilly Wilkerson, Ellsworth Turner; bottom row, left to right: unidentified, James H. Stephenson, Sadie Brooks, Bertha Myers, Julian Jackson. (204-10 thl)

Winchester Evening Star

In the Annual Declamatory Contest held at Storer College last Friday night, the first prize was won by Frances Finley of the Douglas School of Winchester, Va. A great deal of rivalry exists from year to year among the schools of West Virginia, Maryland and Virginia. There is much satisfaction that the trophy has returned to the local school.

Winchester Evening Star
March 16, 1931

The chorus of the Douglas School, Winchester's educational institution for its colored youth, Saturday won first prize in their classification at the 5th Annual Tri-State Contest at Storer College in Harpers Ferry. The chorus was instructed by James Washington who is not a member of the Douglas faculty but a former student there and is also a Storer College graduate. The Winchester chorus competed in the high school group. Members of the chorus are: Dorothy Shields, Alice Weaver, Lucille Finley, Mary Louise Williams, Ida Washington, Mary Cook, Weaver Banks, Yvonne Kirk, Evelyn Saunders, Mary Frances Green, Ellen Williams, Vivienne Jackson, Reginald Mitchell, George Hogan, Jesse Boyd Jr., Charles Williams Jr., Clarence Bannister and Charles Cartwright.

Winchester Evening Star
April 9, 1941

The second and third grades have organized the Courtesy Club. The purpose is to cultivate the habit of courtesy at all time. The pupils are planning to purchase some books for their room library. The officers were: president - Sadie Washington, secretary - Lucille Bland, Mathew Williams - treasurer.

Winchester Evening Star
October 10, 1941

The Science Club was organized again this year with William Beamer as president. The first meeting was used to map out and formulate its program for the year.

Winchester Evening Star
October 18, 1941

A Rainbow Wedding program is beinggiven at 8 o'clock tomorrow evening at the Douglas School on North Kent Street for the benefit of St. Stephens CME Church. Musical numbers will be given also by the Hallelujah Four , a Washington quartette and the Winchester Trio. There will also be an address by Prof. Kirk N. Gaskins, principal of the school.

Winchester Evening Star
October 25, 1941

For the first time in the history of Douglas an Athletic Club has been organized. The club has as its instructor, Thomas Haywood, a new member of the faculty and a recent graduate of Hampton. The club is made up of boys from the 8th through the 11th grade. The purpose of the club is to build more healthy bodies and minds. This club will have boxing as it main feature.

Winchester Evening Star
October 31, 1941

"The Wood Fairies' Halloween" was a play given by the elementary students at the school on Friday night. Three prizes were awarded: Most Original - Marshal Williams 6th grade; Most Beautiful - Thomas Ford 1st grade and Most Comical - Lathan Williams 1st grade.

Winchester Evening Star
November 8, 1941

Defense Stamps are now on sale at the Douglas School in charge of Mrs. Wright. We are asking that Winchester and Frederick County help purchase these stamps. We will publish weekly the names of persons who purchase bonds and stamps.

Winchester Evening Star
Oct 8, 1943

The third grade pupils have been reading poems by Robert Louis Stevenson and are planning an assembly program for Friday, January 21st. Contestants have been chosen for the High School Declamatory Contest to be given in March. They are as follows: Mary Wanzer, Anna Wanzer, Wesley Alsberry, Selma Williams, Alberta Washington, Allene Williams, Bernice Ford, Arthur Gaither, Magdalene Mitchell, Colleen Jackson, Marvel Thompson, Jack Burks and Zelma Pinkett.

Winchester Evening Star
January 21, 1944

Douglas School students, grades second and third, 1944. Front row, left to right: Dorothy Ann Doleman, Joan Allen, Fitzhugh Christian, Barbara Turner, Nancy Grimes, Jean Allen, Lillian Poulsen; second row, left to right: Andrew Gaskins, Charles Brown, Horace Johnson, John Carter Finley, Moses Brown, Kenneth Cooke, Nimrod Turner, Walter Gaither; Third row, left to right: Helen Rhodes, Beverly Richardson, John Ash, unidentified, unidentified, Linwood Williams, Gloria Finley, Ramona Martin, Blanche Gibson Moten (teacher.) (618-6 thl)

Douglas High School students (may be the junior class of 1949) in front of doorway, c. school year 1948-1949. Front row, left to right: Meta Lee Turner, Milbert Taper, Elsie Ford, Joy Gaskins, Beulah Bannister, Sarah Lewis, Mary Fisher; second row, (left to right; Kirk N. Gaskins Sr. (principal), Clifford Brooks, Jr., Richard Ford, Jr., Rosa Gaither, Madison Walker, Nerissa Wright (teacher), Gladys Doleman, Kirk N. Gaskins Jr, Emerson Cooke, Floyd Finley III. (618-5 thl)

Walter Gaither was awarded a prize of one dollar's worth of war savings stamps. He was the winner of the first war stamp contest at Douglas this year.

Winchester Evening Star
January 29, 1944

The amount of stamps bought by the Douglas School students and patorns since December 21, 1943 amounted to 1,365 stamps or $136.50. Mrs. Cartwright has purchased from the school $75.00 worth of stamps and Mr. James F. Robinson has purchased $50.00 worth of stamps.

Winchester Evening Star
February 15, 1944

Negro History Week Continued with programs on February 21 and February 25. Those included on the program include: Anna Wanzer, Taylor Finley Jr., Louis Gaither, James Warren, June Banks, Bernice Ford, Alberta Washington, Lanier Turner, Ellen Williams, and Zelma Pinkett.

Winchester Evening Star
February 19, 1944

The following students were awarded prizes Friday night, March 24th at the Declamation Contest: 1st Prize - Ellen Williams, 2nd Prize - Mary Wanzer, 3rd Prize - Bernice Ford, 4th Prize - Wesley Alsberry, honorable mention - Allene Williams.

Winchester Evening Star
April 15, 1944

The Douglas Glee Club rendered a program Wednesday night at the St. Paul AME Church.

Winchester Evening Star
May 2, 1944

There will be a Popularity Contest given by the Senior Class February 14, 1945. The contestants were chosen from the 4th to the 10th grades inclusive. They are as follows: Fourth Grade, Joan Elliott; Fifth Grade, Ann Ford; Sixth Grade, Doris Catlett; Seventh Grade, Elsie Ford; Eight Grade, Lorraine Cook; Ninth Grade, Audrey Harris and Tenth Grade, Jeanette Grandison.

Winchester Evening Star
November 29, 1944

The children of the first grade gave a Valentine program last Friday under the direction of Miss Layton. The following students were chosen for the High School declamation contest which will be sometime in March: Robert Brooks, Ann Fletcher, Lawrence Finley, James Warren, Grace Blowe, Orissa Taper, Bernice Ford, Selma Williams, William Honesty, Sue Catlett, Charlotte Shields, Audrey Harris, Edward Bartlett, Lanier Turner, Fay Johnson, Louis Gaither, Marvel Thompson, Allene Williams and Helena Pines.

Winchester Evening Star
February 16, 1945

Tuberculosis Education Campaign is now being conducted at the Douglas School under the supervision of Miss E. M. McKinney. The tuberculosis committee for the colored people includes, Dr. John Poulson, Miss E. M. McKinney and the Rev. A. T. Gaskins. The aim of this committee is to win the final battle against this disease.

Winchester Evening Star
April 4, 1945

Henry Phoenix and William Honesty volunteered for the navy and left last Friday morning to take their physical examinations. These were the first two boys who were in regular attendance up until the time of induction to have left Douglas for the service. The faculty presented each with a small New Testament and The Glee Club also presented them with a token.

Winchester Evening Star
April 9, 1945

The winners of the Declamation Contest which was March 23, 1945, are as follows: First prize (tie) Fay Johnson & Bernice Ford, Second prize Coleen Jackson, Third prize Louis Gaither, Fourth prize William Honesty, Honorable Mention Charlotte Shields. The First grade is sponsoring a health program on Friday, April 13 with Dr. John Poulson as the guest speaker.

Winchester Evening Star
April 12, 1945

Douglas School children, c. 1940. Front row, left to right row: David Burks, David Clinton, John C. Finley, Tommy Gaither, Jack Christian, Andrew Gaskins, Hubert Stephenson, Michael Ford, James Prather, Dabney Stephenson, Lathan Williams; second row, left to right; Nancy Grimes, Jean Allen, Marlene Johnson, Joan Allen, Katherine Green, Beverly Long, Loretta Moten, Janet Lewis; third row, left to right: Beverly R. Gaskins, Audrey Willis, Nannie Donnelly, Lillian Poulson, Barbara Turner, Priscilla Bland, Elsie Ford, Shirley Nelson, Eugene Watkins; fourth row, standing in back: Mrs. Blanche Gibson Moten (teacher). (555-8 thl)

Douglas School Students and Teachers - perhaps spring 1952. Kneeling: James Prather; standing, left to right: Richard Pope, Billy Watkins, Nimrod Turner, Alma Louada Layton (teacher), Edward Curry, Charles Jackson with trophy, Mr. Nash (teacher), Irene Wallace (librarian), Eugene Watkins, Basil Puller. (555-140)

Amateur Hour prizes were 1st - The Stephens City Quartet - chocolate cake; 2nd - Andrew Gaskins - lemon cake; 3rd - Joyce Gaskins - lemon pie; and 4th - Zita Laws - apple pie.

Winchester Evening Star
April 27, 1945

The Beta Kappa Chi Scientific Society of Harpers Ferry, W.Va., sponsored a scientific essay contest among twelve high schools in Virginia and West Virginia. The contest was held to create a greater interest in science and to encourage embryo scientists. Douglas School took an active part supervised by Miss E. M. McKinney. We are happy to announce that two of the three winners were students of Douglas: Anna Wanzer 2nd prize and Lanier Turner 3rd prize.

Winchester Evening Star
May 4, 1945

These pupils of the 6th and 7th grades had a lovely trip on Monday, December 10, to the Shenandoah Bank with their teacher, Mrs. Wright. Each one opened a Christmas Savings account and quite a bit of enthusiasm was shown on their part, with bright thoughts for a Merry Christmas in 1946. The students: Lois Wanzer, June Gaskins, Tillie Tracy, Beverly Christian, John Williams, Leon Boles, Franklin Ash and Theodore Ash.

Winchester Evening Star
December 15, 1945

Who will be Miss Douglas? In the running are Josephine Catlett, Fay Johnson, Ann Fletcher, Beulah Bannister, Jane E. Johnson, June Gaskins and Joan Elliot. The ninth grade class will conduct a social at the home of Miss Ann Fletcher, Gibbon Street., in the interest of Miss Douglas, public invited. Refreshments will be for sale.

Winchester Evening Star
March 22, 1946

Douglas School is happy over the news of the coronation of Miss Douglas which is to be held April 5, 1946. The person who is to be Miss Douglas is Josephine Catlett. The amount of money each contestant raised is as follows: Josephine Catlett--$42.50, June Gaskins - $21.80, Ann Fletcher -- $16.55, Beulah Bannister - $15.75, Joan Elliott-- $14.05, Faye Johnson -- $14.00 and Jane Johnson -$5.00 The total amount raised is $129.65 and this is the first time that Douglas School has raised this amount of money.

Winchester Evening Star
April 1, 1946

As a culminating activity on shelter, the Citizenship Club presented a two act play entitled, "Building Our Home." Those who took part are: Nancy Grimes, Shirley Bartlett, Millie Burns, Jean Allen, Lillian Poulson, Joan Allen, Barbara Turner, Bessie Nelson, Mary Jones, Romona Martin, Josephine Smith, Nannie Donley and Marele Wake.

Winchester Evening Star
April 26, 1946

More than 100 children registered at the Douglas School playground. Mrs. Katherine Ford and Miss Sue Catlett will supervise the activities.

Winchester Evening Star
July 8, 1946

A flower show will be held at the Douglas School Playground on Thursday, July 11 at 4:30 p.m. sponsored by the Winchester Recreation Department and assisted by the local colored Girl Scout troops. Ribbons will be awarded for the best arranged cultivated and wildflowers with similar

ribbons awarded for the best single specimen of any flower displayed. Flowers exhibited will later be distributed among the patients of the Winchester Memorial Hospital.

Winchester Evening Star
July 10, 1946

The annual playground doll show was held at the Douglas Playground on Thursday, July 18 at 5:00p.m. Best rag doll, Carol Thomas; best baby doll, June Gaskins, best animal doll, Katherine Greene, best nationality doll, Beatrice Bland.

Winchester Evening Star
July 20, 1946

On Sunday afternoon, August 11, 1946 at 3:00 p.m. the Progressive Mount Olive Chorus of Baltimore, Maryland will present a musical program at the Douglas High School on North Kent Street. This is a chorus of fifty voices under the direction of George S. White with Veronica Bowman accompanist. The proceeds of the concert will be divided between the Negro Day Nursery (now Fremont Street Nursery) and the Junior Missionary Circle of the Mt. Carmel Baptist Church both of Winchester, Virginia.

Winchester Evening Star
August 8, 1946

The Winchester Recreation Department is sponsoring the showing of two motion picture films, Dog Days and Animals in the Service of Man at the Douglas School auditorium at 7:30 tonight. All the patrons and friends of the Douglas Playground children are cordially invited to attend the show.

Winchester Evening Star
August 8, 1946

Douglas School Home Economics class 1964-1965, taught by Lovelena Lomax Marcus. Front row, left to right, Barbara Thompson, Tonya Wheeler, Theresa Carter, Cynthia Martin, Frances Williams, Carolyn Grimes, Barbara Brown; second row, Barbara Grimes, Linda Kay Beamer, Allison FInley, Lovelena Lomax Marcus, Willa Mae Brisco, Augustine Lavender, Lucille Roberts, Phyllis Nelson; third row, Wetzel Jean Weaver, Rebecca Newman, Joanne Jackson, Betty Walker, Claudia Burns, Dorothy Mosee, Joan Walker, Helen Williams, Patricia Bland, Bernice Gant, Cornelia Dorman, Lavenia Jackson, Osceola Shield, Phyllis Washington. (899-9)

CONCERT
DOUGLAS SCHOOL BAND
THURSDAY, APRIL 14, 1960
8:00 P. M.
DOUGLAS SCHOOL AUDITORIUM
WINCHESTER, VIRGINIA

STUDENTS	-	35c
ADVANCE ADULT TICKET	-	60c
AT DOOR	-	50c

For several years, the Douglas High School has had the pleasure of opening its doors to pupils who live out of town. These students bring with them the results of splendid home training and a good wholesale attitude. We feel that our school has been made richer because of the qualities exemplified in the boys and girls.

Winchester Evening Star
October 4, 1946

The Winchester Recreation Department will sponsor a class of Christmas card making in the near future. All persons interested are asked to register or call Douglas School for information. The Junior Red Cross sponsor is glad to report a 100 percent cooperation from the students of Douglas School.

Winchester Evening Star
November 18, 1946

The following students have been elected for the annual Declamatory Contest which will be held this year March 28: Roy Rhodes, Eleanora Cary, Hazel Burks, Thelma Jackson, Sadie Washington, Mary Jackson, Henry Bartlett, William Brown, Ann Cook, Orissa Taper, Lowell Poulson, Jane Johnson, Rosa Gaither, Milbert Taper, Edward Barlett, Emerson Cook, Evelyn Lewis, Joyce Gaskins, Arthur Gaither, Marvel Thompson and Audrey Harris.

Winchester Evening Star
February 17, 1947

The following pupils were prize winners in the High School Declamatory Contest: 1st - Audrey Harris, 2nd - Emerson Cook, 3rd - Joyce Gaskins, Hon. Mention - Evelyn Lewis.

Winchester Evening Star
April 16, 1947

The seventh grade candidates for graduation are as follows: Lucille Bland, Lena Boles, Ann Ford, June Gaskins, Agnes Jackson, Bette Long, Tillie Trace, Helen Turner, Lois Wanzer, Leon Boles, Robert Burks, Paul Burns, Beverly Christian, Richard Christian, Charles Cook, Robert Finley, and James Waldon.

Winchester Evening Star
May 13, 1947

The junior and senior girls have organized a club called, "The Gay Fourtiners," with these officers: Milbert Taper - president Ann Cook -vice president, Orissa Taper - secretary, Elsie Ford - treasurer and Sarah Lewis - sergeant-at-arms. The Glee Club has these officers: Orissa Taper - president, James Waldon - vice president, Rosa Bartlett - secretary, Kenneth Carter - assistant secretary, Wallace Ford - treasurer and Monroe Johnson - sergeant at arms. The directress is Mrs. Anna Tokes and the pianist Mrs. Moten.

Winchester Evening Star
October 3, 1947

Rosa E. Gaither , sixteen year old tenth grade student at the Douglas School , who lives at 656 N. Cameron Street has been judged the winner of the ad-writing contest conducted during the past two weeks by the J. W. Grove Furniture Co. and has been awarded the Englander Bodyguard innerspring mattress which was the announced prize.

Winchester Evening Star
November 13, 1947

The Douglas School tenth graders presented "Red River Gal" a folk dance at assembly program. Taking part were Beulah Bannister, Meta Turner, Milbert Taper, Elsie Ford, Joyce Gaskins, Sarah Lewis, Rosa Gaither and Frances Williams.

Winchester Evening Star
February 16, 1948

A large crowd of music lovers assembled at the Douglas School to hear a program of sacred music given by the youth choir of Asbury Methodist Church of Washington, D.C. The choir was under the direction of Mrs. Eslanda Thomas Cogdell who showed a large degree of skill and training. Mr. Randolph Robinson was chairman of the arrangements.

Winchester Evening Star
December 2, 1948

The senior class at Douglas High School presented Way Back When a play last night at the school auditorium as part of its annual class night. Participants who won prizes in the talent show staged by the Athletic Club were: primary - Benjamin Brown tap dance, Charles and Marshal Gilkerson, musical selections; elementary — Andrew Gaskins solo, Janet Lewis, Josephine Smith and Shirley Nelson trio; high school Joan Elliott and Charles Jackson Spanish dance, Beverly Richardson and Helen Rhodes, Albert Grimes, Edward Curry, Fitzhugh Christian and Walter Gaither tied for first place, Ann Ford solo for second place, Celeste Carter and Franklin Ash guitar duo for third place.

Winchester Evening Star
May 17, 1949

On May 26, the Johnson Williams School of Berryville will present a circus at the Douglas School auditorium at 8:30 p.m. with the public being invited.

Winchester Evening Star
May 17, 1949

Robert Gaither has established himself as checker champion at Douglas playground which has had a record attendance since opening. Lathan Williams is the table tennis champ.

Winchester Evening Star
July 2, 1949

Joy A. Gaskins, Loretta Moten, and June Gaskins in a Douglas School Ballet Show directed by Effie McKinney in 1947. (618-32 thl)

Douglas School students performing Spanish dance in 1952. Left to right: Loretta Moten, Dabney Stephenson, John C. Finley, Eva Marie Marshall, Zita Laws, Edward Curry, Charles H. Jackson, Joan Elliott, James Prather, Helen Curry. Grubbs Studio. (555-104 thl)

Douglas 55

A miniature thatched hut of hand made toothpicks was the oldest curio exhibited at the hobby and curio show held at Douglas playground. It was entered by Mrs. John Woodfolk of 579 N. Kent St. who said an employer gave it to her many years ago. Other winners included Katherine Greene, Tonya Cartwright, Marlene Johnson. In the hobby class, Randall Long won first prize for a bust modeled from clay. Other winners in this class were Robert Gaither and Roy Dendy. James Bartlett won for his Nature Scrap book. Judges were Evelyn Lewis and Doris Catlett.

Winchester Evening Star
July 7, 1949

Last week's activities on Douglas playground were climaxed by a picnic attended by 100 youngsters who played croquet, table tennis, horse shoes and other games before sitting down to hot dogs and other refreshments. James Bartlett was the croquet champion.

Winchester Evening Star
July 12, 1949

Junior Jackson was ping-pong champ last week at Douglas playground. The girls won in softball competition. Charles Grimes is head of the small boys team and Nannie Donnelly, the girls. Harry Myers drilled the Girl Scouts on the playground preparing for the Elk's parade.

Winchester Evening Star
August 3, 1949

The spelling contest sponsored by the Seventh District Virginia teachers' Association was held at the Booker T. Washington High School in Staunton. Winners include: James Parks of Luray, first, Elaine Taylor of Luray, second and Helen Curry of Winchester, third.

Winchester Evening Star
March 23, 1951

The annual Spelling Bee sponsored by the 7th District V.T.A. was held yesterday at the Johnson-Williams High School in Berryville. Mary Frances Carter and Mary Elizabeth Gilkerson, both attending the 7th grade, represented Douglas elementary.

Winchester Evening Star
February 16, 1952

Douglas High School will be the scene of the Elks Oratorical Contest on Friday at 8:30 p.m. Three contestants are entered with the winner going to Alexandria to participate in the District contest. Contestants to vie for two honors and their respective subjects include: James Prather, "Frederick Douglas and the Constitution;" Marlene Wake, "George Washington and the Constitution;" and John Finley, "The Negro and the Constitution."

Winchester Evening Star
March 5, 1953

John Finley, an eleventh grade student at the Douglas School, won the $5.00 prize in the Elk's Oratorical Contest. Second prize winner in Friday's contest was Marlene Wake, a tenth grade student. She was awarded $2.50. Third prize $1.00 went to another tenth grader, James Prather.

Winchester Evening Star
March 10, 1953

Rue Jones of Alexandria was winner in the Elk's District Oratorical Contest. John C. Finley, local contestant of the five entries, placed second. Before the contest, there was a program of entertainment by local talent including a solo by William Gant, a duet by Mary Russell Stephenson and Dulaney Byrd and several songs by the Douglas Glee Club.

Winchester Evening Star
May 6, 1953

A Variety Show featuring talent from schools in Waynesboro, Staunton, Harrisonburg, Elkton, Luray, Berryville and Winchester will be held at the Douglas School auditorium on April 4, at 8 p.m. Benny Brown, well known local tap dancer, will be the guest star of the evening.

Winchester Evening Star
March 28, 1952

The Douglas High School Glee Club directed by Mrs. Laura Turner, will present a musical program at the regular meeting luncheon of the Lions Club to be held at 12 o'clock tomorrow at the George Washington Hotel.

Winchester Evening Star
February 23, 1953

Booker T. Washington's daughter made her visit to the Douglas High School, recently. In her talk to the students, she said that while a college education is important, a skilled trade holds sway in that we must all earn a living. Her talk was along the lines of commercial as well as distributive education as it might service the small business. Parents, faculty members and students of the Douglas School netted $51.25 for the school equipment at the dinner held last Thursday. Some forty-one dinners were served. Funds were added to the amount being used to pay the standard duplicator machine purchased recently.

Winchester Evening Star
February 26, 1953

The forty-four girls and boys of the Douglas School Glee Club, under the direction of Mrs. George Turner Jr., will present a musical program at the Exchange Club to be held at 12:15 p.m. tomorrow at the George Washington Hotel.

Winchester Evening Star
March 23, 1953

Douglas School Glee Club, c. 1945. Front row, seated left to right: Mary Wanzer, Vivian Taper, Audrey Harris, June Banks, Bernice Ford, Allene Williams, Charlotte Shields, Faye Johnson; standing, second row, left to right: Gertrude Cary, Josephine Catlett, Elizabeth Nickens, Selma Williams, Jeanette Grandison, unidentified, Yolanda deNeal, Sue Catlett, Collen Jackson; third row left to right: unidentified, William Honesty, Henry Phoenix, James Carter. (204-11 thl)

Douglas School dancers in 1955. Left to right: Dorothy Curry, Harriet Washington, Ruth Ann Giles, Sandra Finley, Mary Frances Washington, Violet Blowe, Tonya Cartwright. (555-143 wfchs)

The Elk's District Oratorical Contest will be held in the Douglas High School at 3 p.m. Sunday, May 3. John C. Finley, local winner, will compete with representatives of five other Northern Virginia schools.

Winchester Evening Star
April 29, 1953

Officers of the Douglas School Glee Club were elected this week as follows: President, John Finley, Vice-President, Floyd Burks, Secretary & Treasurer, Andy Gaskins, Reporter, James Bartlett and Librarian, Floyd Walker. On December 4, the Glee Club will sing for the Women's Civic League, December 18 for the Lions Club and on December 16 will present a Christmas concert at the Newton D. Baker Hospital near Martinsburg. The Glee Club is composed of fifty-five high school boys and girls. The Glee Club is directed by Mrs. George Turner.

Winchester Evening Star
November 17, 1953

Forty-one prizes were awarded at the Seasonal Fashion Show held by the Modernairs at the Douglas High School on Thursday evening. The judges were Mrs. Charles Snyder and Mrs. Paul Anderson. Miss Effie McKinney was Mistress of Ceremonies and described the clothes worn by models from this city, Frederick County and Millwood. Dean Harris, musical instructor at the Johnson Williams High School in Berryville, led his a-cappella group in several selections.

Winchester Evening Star
December. 8, 1953

The Senior Class of the Douglas High School will present a Fashion Review and Senior Class Wedding tonight at 8 o'clock in the school auditorium. The event will be open to the public. The wedding party will include bride, Loretta Moten, bridegroom, Dabney Stephenson, best man, Floyd Burks, maid of honor, Janet

Lewis, ring bearer, David Finley, flower girls, Cynthia Martin, Helen Walker, Bettina Travis and Wally Ford, bridesmaids, Anna Carter, Jean Allen, Audrey Curry, Zita Laws, Marlene Johnson, Gilbert Carter, Rochella Alsberry and Emma Henderson, ushers, Hubert Stephenson, John Washington, James Stephenson, David Clinton, Alexander Thomas, James Nelson and Roy Cooper. Father of the bride is Michael Ford and the minister is James Carter.

Winchester Evening Star
April 14, 1955

The senior class, for the first time this year, is working on a yearbook, The Doug-Out. Committees for the Doug-Out have been named as follows: art committee, James Carter, chairman, Alexander Thomas, Beverly Gaskins, Mildred Williams and David Clinton; clerical committee all senior girls include Shirley Shields, Elizabeth Jackson, Beverly Long, Rebecca Robinson and Mary Carter. James Bartlett heads the advertising committee. His workers and the areas they are to cover are as follows: Mary Carter, Winchester, James Nickens, Strasburg, Barbara Pye, Woodstock, and Floyd Burks, Middletown.

Winchester Evening Star
October. 28, 1955

On November 3, Dr. William F. Schenck, school dentist, held a clinic at the school. On Thursday, a dinner was held and proceeds will be used for the ninth grade contestant for Miss Homecoming.

Winchester Evening Star
November 5, 1955

The Home Economics class taught by Mrs. Lovelena Marcus sponsored a Thanksgiving dinner at the school on Wednesday for all teachers. We regret the error in the last week's news, saying

it was the first time for the publication of a year book. One was published last year.

Winchester Evening Star
November 29, 1955

During the Thanksgiving holidays, many of our former graduates were home from college. They talked to many of us about their studies and college in general. Their talks were a great encouragement to many students who had decided to quit high school or forget the idea of college. Those students were Marlene Johnson attending St. Phillip's School of Nursing, James Prather and Charles Brown both from Maryland State College, and Dabney Stephenson and Vita Laws from Virginia State College.

Winchester Evening Star
December 3, 1955

The Douglas High School Glee Cub will present its Christmas program December 20, in the school auditorium at 8 p.m. The program, which is free to the public, is under the direction of Tuscan Jasper.

Winchester Evening Star
December 1955

The Douglas Dancing Group has been invited to appear in a Christmas scene for the Dumont Television Company on Christmas Eve. The invitation has been accepted by the instructor of this group, Mrs. Effie McKinney Davis, who will accompany them. The group will appear on Bob McEwen's Capitol Caravan over Channel 5 at 7 p.m. on Christmas Eve. Those in the performance are: Tonya Cartwright, Harriet Washington, Ruth Ann Giles, Frances Washington, Sandra Finley, Violet Blowe and Dorothy Curry. The "Dance of the Bells" will be performed. Also appearing on the program, will be a Douglas alumna, Miss June Gaskins, daughter of Kirk N Gaskins, principal.

Winchester Evening Star
December 18, 1955

SEASONAL
FASHION REVIEW
Douglas High School
WINCHESTER, VIRGINIA

THUR., DEC. 3, 1953
8:00 P. M.

Featuring The Choralairs

Eugene "Johny Ray" Johnson and other talents

Contestants from Numerous Communities will be
Presented

 Sponsored by the Modernairs

Adults 60c - Children 25c

On Tuesday night, the Douglas Glee Club and band, under the direction of Tuscan Jasper, presented a very entertaining Christmas Program at the school.

Winchester Evening Star
December 23, 1955

Mr. Lemley of the Lemley Studio in Stephens City will take pictures of the entire school and faculty January 16, at 9:00 am. The seniors are not expecting their class rings until March. They are awaiting the occasion with great anxiety.

Winchester Evening Star
January 16, 1956

Subscriptions are now being solicited for the yearbook, The Doug-Out. All members of the senior class are taking orders. Get your book ordered early!

Winchester Evening Star
January 27, 1956

The Douglas School Glee Club will leave Saturday, March 17, for Shell, Virginia, where they will render a musical program in the Northern Virginia Musical Festival. The local group consists of thirty-five male and female voices. Tuscan Jasper is director of music at the school. All groups participating will be judged and awards will be made for the highest ranking organization. There will be judging for both instrumental and voice. Funds for transportation for the local group are being contributed by the Winchester Lions Club.

Winchester Evening Star
March 2, 1956

Six members of the Salvation Army Advisory Board spoke to a recent assembly period at the Douglas School and on Wednesday, some 56 members of the junior and senior class of the school were taken on a tour of Salvation Army headquarters. Each pupil will write an essay on the local work of the Salvation Army. A $50.00 Savings Bond will be awarded to the writer of the best essay in the 11th grade at each of the five area high schools.

Winchester Evening Star
March 1956

On Monday April 16, at 8 p.m., there will be a Fashion Show and Musical at the Douglas School auditorium sponsored by the New Homemakers of America and the Douglas Glee Club. The teachers for these two groups are: Mrs. Lovelena Marcus and Mr. Tuscan Jasper.

Winchester Evening Star
March 12, 1956

The senior class of the Douglas School will serve a turkey dinner in the home-making department tomorrow beginning at 5 p.m. The dinner is open to everyone and home deliveries will be made upon request.

Winchester Evening Star
April 18, 1956

The Senior Class will present an Oratorical Contest May 9, at the Douglas High School. The program will consist of an oration by each member of the class. The Junior-Senior Prom will be held May 11, in the high school gymnasium. Mrs. R. M. Barksdale and C. F. Dendy are sponsors of the prom and the junior class.

Winchester Evening Star
May 1, 1956

The NHA Chapter of the Douglas High School will sponsor a fried chicken dinner including desert, Thursday, beginning at 4:30 p.m. Dinners will be served at the school or delivered upon request.

Winchester Evening Star
May 22, 1956

On Thursday from 8– 10 p.m., The Home Economics and Industrial Arts Departments of the Douglas High school will hold open house. The event will be open to the public. There will be an exhibition of articles made in both departments. The dinner held last week was most successful.

Winchester Evening Star
May 29, 1956

The Annual Honor's Day was held in the school auditorium Friday. Charles F. Dendy, the chairman of the Athletic council was master of ceremonies. The outstanding members of the Senior Class were awarded the following honors: Elizabeth Jackson for receiving the valedictorian and senior girl athletics, Rebecca Robinson for the best all around senior, Mildred Williams was awarded the title of honor student of the class, James Bartlett claimed the award for leadership in the senior class, and Floyd Burks received an honor for senior boy athletics. The Senior Class presented a departmental gift of two sets of blue willow china with a place setting of sixteen to Mrs. Lovelena Marcus the instructor of the Home Economics Department.

Winchester Evening Star
June 7, 1956

The Junior Class of the Douglas High School will present the Harmonizing Four of Richmond in recital here Tuesday evening. The program to be held in the auditorium of the Douglas School will start promptly at 8:15 p.m.

Winchester Evening Star
November 3, 1956

Douglas High School Glee Club, 1958-59. Front row, left to right: Patricia Tolliver, Maxine Blowe, Charlotte Virginia Corley, Ann Ranson, Edna Allen, Dorothy Curry, Arnetta Lavender, Carolyn Gaither, Barbara Williams, Julia Brown, Gloria Gaither, Closia Gene King, Violet Blowe; second row, left to right: Brenda Bundy, Tonya Cartwright, Ellen Delores Dyer, Mary Frances Washington, Judy Gaither, Zellene Long, Dorothy Scott, Sandra Finley, Katherine Gaither, Sylvia Washington, Sharon Williams, Jackie Williams, Harriet Washington; third row, left to right: Kenneth Burks, Austin Crawford, Jerome Jackson, Lawrence Carter, James Walker, Albert Delaney Long, Jack Brown, Lawrence Gaskins, Augustus Gaskins, James Brown, Paul Walker, Garland Williams. (599-60 thl)

The Raging Tornados Jazz Band included students from Douglas High School. (1493-5 thl)

The Primary Department Grades 1-4, at the Douglas School will present a Christmas operetta Wednesday evening at 8 o'clock at the school. The operetta is entitled Don't Tell Me Its Christmas. The program is under the direction of Mrs. Mattie Cross, Mrs. Blanche Moten, Mr. Tuscan Jasper and Mrs. Hester Harris.

Winchester Evening Star
December 15, 1956

On January 7, the student body of the Douglas High School went to the Winchester-Frederick County Health Department to receive their polio shots.

Winchester Evening Star
January 15, 1957

The Senior Class of Douglas School recently observed National Education Week. The theme around which the discussions evolved was "We Learn Not for School, But for Life." Mrs. Effie Davis organized and directed this program.

Winchester Evening Star
November 21, 1957

The news in a nutshell around Douglas is that Margaret Jackson, Beverly Harris and Josephine Gant, senior girls, have entered the Lennox table setting contest. The Douglas Glee Club will present a spring concert at the school auditorium April 24. The public is cordially invited to come out and give the Glee Club its full support. Congratulations to Barbara Williams and Harriet Washington who represented Douglas in the Dramatic Festival last Friday. They placed first and second respectively in the Oratorical Contest held in Staunton.

Winchester Evening Star
April 18, 1958

A farce comedy in three acts entitled *It's A Great Life* will be presented by the Senior Class May 8, at 8:15 p.m. in the school auditorium. The play is filled with humor and rapid clever dialogue that will make you gleefully shout, "It's A Great Life."

Winchester Evening Star
May 5, 1958

Jack Brown was elected president of the Douglas School Senior Class at its first meeting. Other officers are: Ann Ransom, vice president; Sylvia Washington, secretary; Augustus Gaskins, treasurer and Marshall Nickens, business manager. Candidates have been selected also for Miss Homecoming as follows: eighth grade, Violet Blowe; ninth grade, Arnetta Lavender; tenth grade, Patricia Tolliver; eleventh grade, Harriet Washington; twelth grade, Katherine Gaither. This year's edition of the Doug Out is being prepared for publication.

Winchester Evening Star
October 1958

The Douglas High School music department will present a Christmas Recital Sunday at 8:00 p.m. in the school auditorium. The concert will feature the combined choirs of the Page Jackson of Charles Town, West Virginia and Douglas High School. A silver offering will be taken at the door.

Winchester Evening Star
December 13, 1958

The Douglas High school Glee Club will sing at St. Paul A.M.E. Church tomorrow at 8:00 p.m. sponsored by the C.F.D. Club. Reverend J. C. Gordon is pastor of the church and the service is open to the public.

Winchester Evening Star
December 1958

The senior class has been very busy making preparations for Douglas' first Student Council under the supervision of Mrs. Ruth Barksdale.

Winchester Evening Star
January 16, 1959

At school this week it is very exciting. The Senior Class has organized a Student Council. It is a success in school and is contributing a great deal.

Winchester Evening Star
January 31, 1959

The members of the Glee Club journeyed to Culpeper on Saturday to the State Music Festival. There were seventeen Glee Clubs present. This year, Douglas is with District 1 group, whereas last year, we were placed with District 2. In April, we are hoping to attend the music concert in Middleburg.

Winchester Evening Star
March 14, 1959

The Douglas School junior class will sponsor a turkey dinner Thursday beginning at 5:00 p.m. The menu will include turkey, dressing, gravy, sweet potatoes, green beans, sauerkraut, cranberry sauce, rolls and cake.

Winchester Evening Star
March 31, 1959

The junior Class of Douglas High School will present a fashion show entitled, "Twenty Four Hours of Fashion with Vogue" Monday at 8 p.m. in the school auditorium. Mrs. Ruth Barksdale, junior class sponsor, is directing the project. Boys and girls from each class in school will model latest fashions for school, sports, parties, evening and bedtime.

Winchester Evening Star
April 11, 1959

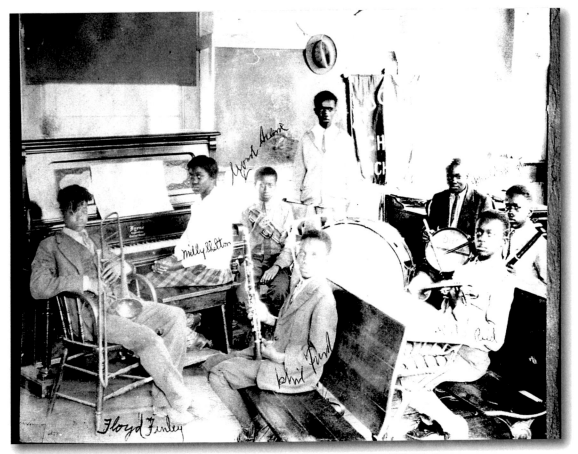

Eight members of the Douglas School band, c. 1910. Floyd Finley, trombone, Milly Shelton, piano, Phil Ford clarinet, John Washington, snare drum, Charles Reed, trumpet, others are unidentified. They would practice on the fourth floor of Rouss City Hall. (555-5 thl)

Douglas High School Marching Band sitting in stands at the Douglas vs. Cardozo football game in November 1962. (204-74a)

Home Economics pupils at the Douglas School will have a turkey dinner this evening. Lemon tarts were listed as the desert.

Winchester Evening Star
October 15, 1959

Two seniors at Douglas, Tonya Cartwright and Harriet Washington, gave detailed reports of Booker T. Washington Girl's State held in Richmond in July to members of Conrad Hoover Unit #21 American Legion Auxiliary on Tuesday. Miss Cartwright and Miss Washington told of the instruction in government they received and expressed their thanks to the ladies auxiliary for sending them:

Winchester Evening Star
October 17, 1959

The play, The Bridal Chamber or Winnie the Miss, will be presented at Douglas School tomorrow at 8 p.m.

Winchester Evening Star
October 21, 1959

Annual Career Day, sponsored by the Winchester-Frederick County Teacher's Association was held at the Douglas School here on Friday. The Seniors from Johnson-Williams School, Berryville, and the parents of the juniors and seniors also attended. The program consisted of consultation sessions, an assembly program, luncheon and a tea which climaxed the day's activities.

Winchester Evening Star
March 1, 1960

The Douglas High School band participated in the Northern Regional Band Festival in Warrenton Saturday. The band was just organized this year and is very proud of the two plus rating that it received. The Glee Club will go to Charlottesville, March 28, to the Northern Regional Musical Festival. On April 7, the Glee Club will present its annual recital. The band will present its first concert on April 14. Both groups are under the direction of Tuscan Jasper.

Winchester Evening Star
March 24, 1960

Four Douglas students, Betty Payne, Gloria Gaither, Wallee Ford and Jacqueline Williams represented their Library Club at the annual conference of Virginia Student Library Assistants Association at Virginia State College, Petersburg; April 9th. The conference consisted of a panel discussion, special sessions for student assistants and others.

Winchester Evening Star
April 14, 1960

Under the gifted baton of conductor, Tuscan Jasper, the Douglas Concert Band held its first annual concert in the school auditorium last night. Impressive as a performance by a high school group could be expected, this one was even more so when taken into consideration that this is the students first year together. At intermission, plaques were presented to State Senator, Harry F. Byrd, Jr, editor of the Winchester Evening Star and Charlie Tate, sports editor for the paper for outstanding news and sports coverage.

Winchester Evening Star
April 5, 1960

The Douglas High School Band and Glee Club will present a concert at St. Paul's AME Church tomorrow at 8 p.m. The event is being sponsored by the St. Paul Improvement Committee.

Winchester Evening Star
April 21, 1960

Harriet Washington, who spoke on Good Citizen Under the Constitution, placed first in the Elks annual oratorical contest at the Douglas School. Runner up was Tonya Cartwright. The first place winner will go to the regional contest in Alexandria.

Winchester Evening Star
May 2, 1960

Harriet Washington, Douglas salutatorian and winner of the local Elk'soratorical contest, placed second in the state contest in Richmond.

Winchester Evening Star
May 21, 1960

The Douglas School senior class will present the mystery comedy, *Lights Out*, at the school auditorium tomorrow at 8:30 p.m.

Winchester Evening Star
June 1, 1960

Following commencement exercises at Douglas High Tuesday night, the 500 guests visited the school's gym to see hundreds of exhibits completed the boys in their shop program this year.

Winchester Evening Star
June 9, 1960

There will be a banquet in the Douglas High School Gymnasium on December 2, 8:30 p.m. sponsored by the Band Boosters Club. Entertainment will be furnished by the Douglas Glee Club and the Douglas School Band.

Winchester Evening Star
November 19, 1960

Douglas School majorettes at a game on Douglas Field c.1960. Left to right: Jacqueline Williams, Virginia Ann Washington, Betty Jo Payne. (555-100 thl)

Douglas School students getting ready for band practice on September 13, 1961. Left to right: Sharon Williams, Christine Brooks, Anna Mae Walker, Virginia Ann Washington, Betty Jo Payne. (204-79c thl)

Douglas 65

Tuscan Jasper, director, (on the far right) with the Douglas High School Band in 1962. (599-1 thl)

Pupils at the Douglas school have contributed $27.00 to the March of Dimes. The students of both the elementary and high school departments attended basketball games at the activity period in order to raise money for the March of Dimes. The games were played by the nineth grade Tree toppers and the eleventh grade Woodstock Flyers. Both games were won by the Tree toppers.

Winchester Evening Star
January 28, 1961

Douglas Band and Glee Club get top rating. The band festival was at the John J. Wright School at Shell and the Glee Club Festival was held at Parker Gray High in Alexandria. Performances in both festivals were rated according to eight different categories and the Douglas groups were given top ratings in both events. Tuscan Jasper directs both the band and the glee club.

Winchester Evening Star
April 1, 1961

The nineth and tenth grades at Douglas are sponsoring a combination skit and comedy night at the school gym tomorrow beginning at 7:30 p.m. Proceeds from the occasion will go toward a trip to Washington for the youngsters where they will visit the National Zoological Park, and other points of interest. All the activities are for girls and boys and include basketball, tumbling and volleyball, a dance routine and the girls m

Winchester Evening Star
April 11, 1961

The Douglas High School Glee Club will present its annual spring concert on Sunday at 8 p.m. in the school auditorium. As a finale, the Glee Club will be accompanied by the band in a setting of the 150th Psalm by Caesar Franck transcribed for band and choir b Reynolds. The Douglas group has been rated by the state of Virginia as a Group I choir.

Winchester Evening Star
April 10, 1962

Among the 147 high school students to participate in the All State Band Festival at Virginia State College in March were eleven students from Douglas High School. Sidney Hodkinson of the University of Virginia was selected by the Music Conference of the Virginia Teacher's Association as the guest conductor for the three day program. Local members participating were: Charles Finley (1st coronet), George Anthony (1st trombone), Joseph Willis (tuba), Herman Jackson (baritone horn), Lucien Bannister (tympani), Barbara Thompson (1st clarinet), Linda Beamer (1st clarinet), Phyllis Washington (2nd clarinet), Elizabeth Walker (bass clarinet.)

Winchester Evening Star
April 10, 1963

The Douglas School Glee Cub will present its annual Spring Concert Sunday in the school auditorium at 4 p.m. The Glee Club will be joined by the Shenandoah Choral Society and the Douglas Band for several numbers. As a finale to the program the Glee Club will be joined by the other two groups and will perform the Battle Hymn of the Republic by Ringwald. The guest conductor of the afternoon will be Lawrence Gaskins, a former student at the school.

Winchester Evening Star
April 10, 1963

In collaboration with the celebration of both American Education Week and National Children's Book Week, the Library Club at Douglas sponsored a Faculty Tea and Educational Film Forum on Tuesday in the school library. Members of the Library Club are as follows: Phyllis Washington, president, Frances Carter, vice president, Cecily Byrd, secretary, Kay Beamer, assistant secretary, Willla Brisco, treasurer, Margaret Green, parliamentarian and Priscilla Rodgers, reporter. Other members are Georgia Kane, Allison Finley, Barbara Thompson, Betty Walker, Charlena Washington, Irvin Baltimore, Herman Jackson, Randolph Martin and Richard Williams. Miss Inez Mercer was their sponsor.

Winchester Evening Star
November 15, 1963

Douglas High site of exams for scholarship – Winchester will be one of 33 Virginia centers offering examinations to high school students seeking admissions or scholarship awards among United Negro College Fund institutions next year. This program is conducted annually as an education service of the United Negro College Fund and expects to test up to 15,000 students from more than 1,500 high schools.

Winchester Evening Star
November 27, 1963

Miss Cynthia E. Martin was elected to be correspondent to the Co-Ed Magazine at the regular meeting of the Douglas High School Homemakers' Club. This job is offered schools having twenty or more subscriptions to the magazine. Miss Sheila D. Humbert, because of her deep interest in clothing, was accepted by McCalls as a member of their Teen Fashion Board. The Homemakers' Club is also planning a play to be presented the latter part of February or early in March.

Winchester Evening Star
January 10, 1964

The Music Department of Douglas High School will present its Concert Band in recital tomorrow at 8 p.m. in the school auditorium. The band, under the direction of Mr. Tuscan Jasper, will perform nine selections. The concert is free and open to the public.

Winchester Evening Star
May, 1964

The 1964-1965 Douglas School Marching Band standing outside the school. Glen Gore, band director, is standing on the far right. Kneeling in front of drums: Linda Long; kneeling left to right, (drums): Edward Jackson, Wesley Thompson Jr, Thomas Gaither, George Gaither, Norman Blowe, George Dixon, Wesley Brooks, Irvin Baltimore, Ronald Nelson, Robert Brooks; Second row, left to right: Judy Humbert, Barbara Brown, Elizabeth Harris, Sylvia Washington, Tonya Wheeler, Barbara Grimes, unidentified, Peggy Nelson, Gail Christian, Debbie Lavender, Patricia Bland, Carolyn Grimes, Linda Williams, Debbie Bundy, Helen Williams, Allison Finley; third row, left to right Elizabeth Harris, Joseph Harris, unidentified, Robert Burks, Glen Ford, unidentified, Helena Butler, unidentified. (555-41 thl)

Lorraine Cook, "Miss Douglas 1945," with Kirk N. Gaskins Sr (principal), David Burks, Jean Carol Finley, Joan Elliot and Ann Ford at Douglas High School's Coronation of Miss Douglas. (204-14)

Douglas High School 1949 Homecoming Queen "Miss Douglas," cheerleaders and faculty. Front row, left to right: Gloria Finley, Sarah Burns, Nannie Donnelly, Lillian Poulsen, June Gaskins, Helen Rhodes, Barbara Turner, Jean Alexander, Effie M. McKinney (teacher); second row, left to right: Ann Ford, Rosalie Bartlett, Fitzhugh Christian (Queen), Powell Willard Gibson (retired principal), Shirley Bartlett. (618-7)

Douglas High School Homecoming 1951. Left to right: Jack Brown, Brenda Bundy, Shirley Shields, Joan Elliott (queen), June Gaskins, Helen Curry, Joan Brown, Tonya Cartwright, Austin Crawford Jr. (555-142)

Douglas High School 1953 Homecoming Queen and Court. Left to right: Jean Allen, Brenda Bundy, Elizabeth Jackson, Patricia Finley (Queen), Audrey Curry, Sylvia Stephenson, Annie Shields (1952 Queen). (618-26)

Douglas High School Homecoming 1955. Left to right: Nancy Davis, Mildred Williams, David Clinton, Jean Carol Finley (queen), Rebecca Robinson, Floyd Burks, Mary Carter, Beverly Sue Harris. (555-144)

Douglas High School 1957 Homecoming Queen and court. Left to right: Randolph "Rannie" Carter, Sandra Lee Finley, Ann Ranson (Queen), Jacqueline "Jackie" Williams, Ruth Ann Giles, Garland Williams. (599-5)

Douglas High School Homecoming 1959-60 Left to right: Wanda Clifford, George Curry Jr., Melvin Cooper, Charlotte Virginia Corley (queen), Ronald Moten, Clifford Lee Mason, Charles Corley, Ellen Delores Dyer. This was a Douglas unbeaten, untied, unthreatened season. Douglas scored 136 total points, opponents only scored 7. (555-141)

Douglas High School Homecoming November 12, 1960. Queen Maxine Blowe (right), and Dorothy Scott (left) Date estimated as early 1960s. (1710-1b)

HOMECOMING QUEEN

Douglas High School Homecoming 1958. Queen Harriet Washington

Miss Harriet Washington

Douglas High School cheerleaders at the Douglas vs. Cardoza, football game in November 1962. Left to right: Judy Humbert, Constance Jackson, Joanne Lavender, Ann Harris, Linda Long, Julia Brown. (204-77)

Douglas High School band at 1960 Homecoming. (599-2)

The Junior Class
of
Douglas High School
requests your presence at their
Junior and Senior Prom
Friday, May 29, 1964   8:30 to 1:00 a.m.
to be held at
Douglas High School Gymnasium
Music by Bob Marshall and the Crystals

Present Invitation at Door

DANCE CARD

Junior and Senior Prom

1952

D H S

Douglas High School Prom in 1956. Janet Lewis in her prom dress. (555-40 thl)

Douglas School show in 1956. Left to right: Beverly Sue Harris, Phyllis Clifford, James Bartlett, Anna Strother, and Patricia Finley. (555-103 thl)

Douglas High School prom of 1959. Front row, left to right: Frank Jackson, Tonya Cartwright, Wanda Clifford, Jean Allen, Barbara Williams, Charlotte Virginia Corley, Harriet Washington, Nancy Davis, Ellen Delores Dyer, Theodore Tolliver; second row, left to right: Charles Corley, Bushrod Harris, Ronald Moten, Melvin Cooper, Frank Lavender, Clifford Lee Mason, Carter Alsberry. (599-4 thl)

The home economics and shop (industrial arts) classes gather together at Douglas High School, during 1958 Senior Prom. Front row, left to right: Charles Finley, Leroy Woodson, Robert Shields, Charles Washington, George Anthony, Robert Jackson, Charles Jackson; second row, left to right: Zellene Long, Sandra Finley, Arnetta Lavender, Dorothy Curry, Carolyn Gaither, Theodore Tolliver, George Curry, Joseph Shields, Clifford Lee Mason; third row, left to right: John Alsberry, Kenneth Pye, Eugene Polston, Moses Long, Melvin Cooper, Stanley Long, James Elwood Walker, Jerome Jackson, Robert Cooper, Albert Delany Long, Paul Williams. (599-21 thl)

James Walker and Barbara Williams at the 1958 Douglas High School Prom. (555-152 wfchs)

DECLAMATION CONTEST   CORONATION MISS DOUGLAS "45"

PROGRAM

Colleen Jackson
> The Negro Has a Chance   anonymous

Ana Wanzer
> Keeping His Word   anonymous

Audrey Harris
> Trouble in the Amen Corner   T. E. Harbaugh

Selma Williams
> A Legend of Brogenz   Adelaide A. Proctor

Bernice Ford
> The Polish Boy   Ann S. Stephens

William Honesty
> The Scar   A. L. Layton

Selection Glee Club   Steal Away

Lorraine Cook
> The Wreck of the Hesperus   Longfellow

Fay Johnson
> Curfew Must Not Ring Tonight   Thorpe

Louis Gaither
> Gone With a Handsomer Man   Will Carleton

Allene Williams
> The Changling   J.G. Whittier

Charlotte Shields
> Poor Little Joe   D. L. Proudfit

Sue Catlett
> The Party   Paul L. Dunbar

Selection Glee Club   An Irish Lullaby

Decision of Judges. . . Mr. Easley, Mrs. Door, Miss Estelle Mitchell, Dr. T. F. Finley, Rev. A. Gaskins

CORNATION MISS DOUGLAS "45"

REFRESHMENTS FOR SALE

School Athletics

Douglas School Athletics

Sporting programs played a big part in the life of Douglas students. The Douglas Bulldogs were known throughout Virginia, West Virginia and Maryland as powerhouse teams and enjoyed many winning seasons. The teams practiced hard, obeyed their coaches' instructions and enjoyed the comradery with fellow students. The Douglas teams were the pride of the community and always played to a packed house.

Douglas Athletic Association. Douglas School faculty mid-1950s. Front row, left to right: Dorothy Dandridge, Mattie Russell, Kirk N. Gaskins, Sr. (principal), Carrie Hines, Ruth Barksdale; second row, left to right: Francis M. Jackson, Hester Harris, Henry Moss Brooks, Effie M. McKinney, Tuscan Jasper, Edwin K. Barksdale. (555-73a)

Douglas School baseball team, Winchester, Virginia. Some of the players are: Joe Long (coach), Willard Gibson and Leon Boles. Photo taken at the Douglas School on Piccadilly Street c. 1925. (1493-50)

Douglas High School Winchester, Virginia 1954-55 Basketball Team John Carter, Robert Burks, Hubert Stephenson, Dabney Stephenson, Michael Ford, James Prather, Coach Barksdale and Beverly Gaskin

Douglas High School 1954-1955 basketball team. Front row, left to right: Robert Burks, Dabney Stephenson w/trophy, James Prather w/basketball, Beverly Gaskins; second row, left to right: John Carter, Hubert Stephenson, Michael Ford, Coach Edwin K. Barksdale. (555-77c)

Winchester Evening Star

Now that we have basketball in our school, the girls, too, have organized two teams under the names of the Speeders and they are as follows: Alberta Washington - Captain, Vivian Taper, Lavinia Martin, Grace Carter, Ruth Spencer, Vivienne Jackson, Mary Williams, and Alice Crawford. The Cossacks – Gertrude Cary - captain, June Banks, Hanniah Cary, Zelma Pinkett, Selma Williams, Mary Armstead, Mary Wanzer, Margretta Gaithers.

Winchester Evening Star
January 22, 1943

The Winchester Red Sox is a newly organized ball club composed of the members of Douglas and outsiders. This team took a defeat at the hands of the Berryville team on Easter Monday. The Red Sox are planning for a good season this year and are expecting a return game with Berryville in the near future.

Winchester Evening Star
April 15, 1944

There will be on Sunday, May 7, a ball game between the Winchester Red Sox and Berryville. This is a return game and will be played at the Lucy Brown Park on Front Royal Road.

Winchester Evening Star
May 6, 1944

Our football team, recently organized, is progressing nicely. Rev. Gaskins, who has been coaching these boys, seems well pleased with the interest manifested. We appreciate the generosity of the local athletic club which has permitted us to use their equipment for the season.

Winchester Evening Star
November 9, 1945

The Douglas School football team will play its initial game in Martinsburg on Saturday, November 17, at 2:30 pm.

Winchester Evening Star
November 17, 1945

The Football team of Douglas School had pictures taken on Tuesday. The captain of the team is Jack Burks.

Winchester Evening Star
December 21, 1945

Mr. Jackson, our conductor of the field day activities, is inviting the schools of Cooksville, Frederick, Rockville, Martinsburg, Berryville and other near-by schools to take part in a Field Day to be held at Douglas School in Winchester, Va., May 10th at 10:00 sharp. Some of the events are dodgeball, dashes, broad jump, high jump, relays and softball.

Winchester Evening Star
April 12, 1946

Douglas High School's Boy and Girls track and field teams finished first in the Tri-State Association meet here. The local team tallied 79 points, followed by Martinsburg with 20 and Berryville with 7 points. Setting the scoring pace for the local teams were Edward Bartlett, Marvel Thompson, Arthur Gaither, Dorothy Doleman, Evelyn Lewis, James Waldon and Wallace Ford.

Winchester Evening Star
May 15, 1947

Coach Francis M. Jackson and a squad of about thirty boys and girls from Douglas will travel by bus to Charles Town on Friday for the third annual Tri-State Track Meet. The local teams will be out to retain a championship won at last year's meet here. Douglas placed third in the 1946 meet. Among the schools competing in the Friday meet will be Winchester, Leesburg and Berryville, Virginia; Frederick, Cumberland, Hagerstown, Lockville and Cooksburg, Maryland and Martinsburg, Piedmont and Charles Town, West Virginia.

Winchester Evening Star
April 20, 1948

Douglas School placed third behind Rockville and Charles Town in the Tri-State track meet at Charles Town. Scoring gave Rockville 90 points, Charles Town 48 and Winchester 34. Martinsburg was fourth.

Winchester Evening Star
April 29, 1948

Douglas High School 1956-1957 basketball team. Front row, left to right: John B. Brown, John Carter, James Walker, Clifford Lee Mason; second row, left to right: Thomas Washington, Raymond Blowe, James Stephenson, Ronald Moten; third row, left to right: Coach Edwin K. Barksdale, James Carter, John Spencer, Frank Lavender. (555-77d)

Douglas High School 1957-1958 basketball team. From row, left to right Edwin K. Barksdale (coach), James Walker, Ronald Moten, Thomas Washington, John Spencer; second row, Kenneth Burks, Raymond Blowe, Clifford Lee Mason, George Curry, John Benjamin Brown, and Stanley Long.

Douglas High School finished the grid season with a record of two wins and two losses. Under the direction of Coach Charles Dendy, they swamped the Williams Training team of Berryville twice, losing twice to Charles Town High school. Boys who have played their last season for Douglas are Richard Ford Jr., Kirk Gaskins Jr., Clifford Brooks Jr., William Brown and Emerson Cook.

Winchester Evening Star
December 7, 1948

On the basketball squad are Kirk N. Gaskins Jr., Clifford Brooks Jr., Leon Boles, Richard Ford, Charles Jackson, Henry Bartlett, Emerson Cook, Celesta Carter, Alvin Carter, Roy Rhodes, William Brown, Harry Brown and Paul Burns.

Winchester Evening Star,
December 18, 1948

Pushing over three touchdowns in the final quarter, the Douglas school six man football team defeated Ramer Memorial High School at Martinsburg 33-21. Grimes paced the winner's offensive with four 6 pointers. Also in the backfield for Douglas was Burns with Carter, Rhodes and Curry on the line.

Winchester Evening Star
October 18, 1949

The Douglas Bulldogs, a throw back to the Tri-State 48 champions, romped to a convincing 52-23 triumph over the Ramer High School of Martinsburg, West Virginia yesterday. A Homecoming day crowd of 500 saw the hard driving Bulldogs come from behind and score twice in the first half to take a lead of 14 to 6 never to be over taken again.

Winchester Evening Star
October 29, 1949

A powerful Douglas High School football team maintained its unblemished 1949 record yesterday by overrunning Page Jackson High School of Charlestown, West Virginia 27-2 before a crowd of 400. The victory was the sixth straight for Coach Charles Dendy's Winchester six.

Winchester Evening Star
November 5, 1949

Douglas High School football squad will go into action for the first time this year when the Bulldogs entertain the Douglas Alumni at 2 p.m. Thursday. For the first time in Douglas' recent history its football team will play the eleven-man game. This might not be Douglas' best season but it could be the most concentrated.

Winchester Evening Star
September. 25, 1950

The Bulldogs won their second victory by defeating Charles Town, West Virginia by a score of 25-2. Waldon, the brains of last year's Bulldogs, will be calling the signals again this year.

Winchester Evening Star
October 17, 1950

Record of the Bulldogs so far is two losses and two wins. They bowed to Cumberland 25-19; beat their Alumni 25-19. Whipped Charlestown, West Virginia 25-2 and lost to Harpers Ferry 19-7. A member of their backfield has won a scholarship to Storer College in Harpers Ferry. He is quarterback James Waldon who graduates in June of next year.

Winchester Evening Star
October 24, 1950

The Douglas High School Bulldogs won an easy victory over the Cumberland Bears last Friday with a score of 26-6.

Winchester Evening Star
October 30, 1950

The Douglas Bulldogs were defeated by the Manassas Bulldogs last Thursday in Manassas, Virginia. This game is not included in the Tri-State League. Carver High School in Cumberland, Maryland and Douglas High School are neck in neck for first place in the Tri-State League. The Homecoming game at Douglas will be played November 15th. Roy Rhodes, Paul Burns and James Waldon will be playing their last game with the Bulldogs.

Winchester Evening Star
November 6, 1950

The Douglas Bulldogs closed the football season with a very colorful Homecoming Day Celebration. June Gaskins took honors in becoming Miss Homecoming of 1950 while Lillian Poulson ran a close second. Although the Bulldogs were defeated in the last quarter, we praise them and the coach for their very good performance during this football season.

Winchester Evening Star
November 18, 1950

Coach Dendy showed his appreciation to the football boys last Thursday with a chicken dinner.

Winchester Evening Star
December 16, 1950

86

James Elwood Walker (right) received the basketball trophy from Coach Edwin K. Barksdale in 1958. (555-153b)

Douglas High School 1959 boys' basketball team. Left to right: Kenneth Pye, Clifford Lee Mason, George Curry, Frank Lavender, Ronald Moten, Melvin Cooper, James Walker, Robert Washington, Webster Washington, John Laws Jr., Bushrod Harris, Stanley Long. (555-77a)

In their second game of the season the Douglas High School Bulldogs face the Johnson Williams Hornets of Berryville at 7:30 p.m. tonight in the Winchester Armory. The Bulldogs who dropped their opener with Leesburg 48-24 are scheduled to play in the local armory every Thursday throughout January and February.

Winchester Evening Star
January 11, 1951

Going up against the undefeated untied North Street Colored High School of Hagerstown, Maryland, the Douglas Bulldogs were trounced on the Armory court here last night. It was the third defeat for the Winchester team which has collected one victory out of four starts this season.

Winchester Evening Star
January 19, 1951

The Douglas Colored High School Bulldogs lost their tilt 63-32 last night against the Howard Cagers of Piedmont, West Virginia in a game on the latter's home court. Scorers on the Douglas team include: B. Christian, C. Jackson, J. Waldon, E. Curry, A. Grimes, P. Burns, C. Boles, K. Cook, N. Turner, E. Watkins.

Winchester Evening Star
January 24, 1951

The Douglas Colored High School Bulldogs team won two out of three games played last night in the Winchester Armory tripping up Andrew Jackson of Luray 32-29, humbling the Luray girls 26-10 but losing to the Page Jackson quintet from Charles Town by 25-15. Sharing in the victory, the Douglas girls whipped the visiting team paced by Joan Allen's 9 markers and the 6 taken by Barbara Turner.

Winchester Evening Star
January 26, 1951

The Douglas Colored School of Winchester was out-pointed 45-38 last night in Leesburg by the defending Douglass School team of that city.

Winchester Evening Star
February 14, 1951

Against Johnson Williams of Berryville on Tuesday, the Winchester quintet took the decision 50-37 on the Clarke County court as did the Douglas JVs by one point at 17-16. James Waldon of the Bulldogs scored 18, followed by E. Watkins and T. Cook with 10 apiece.

Winchester Evening Star
February 22, 1951

The Douglas High School Bulldogs won their home tilt here in the Winchester Armory last night 39-36 from the visiting Sanders team from Moorefield, West Virginia. Taking top scoring honors for the evening was James Waldon of the Bulldogs, his seven goals and a single foul shot, gaining him 15. Following were Ed Curry with 10 and E. Watkins who got 8.

Winchester Evening Star
March 2, 1951

In their Saturday game with the Lincoln Colored High School cagers of Rockville, Maryland, the visiting Douglas Bulldogs squeaked past the home team by one point 42-41. Sparking the Bulldogs was E. Curry, who took six field goals and both of his free throws for 14, followed by J. Waldon with 13 giving the visitors top scoring honors for the event.

Winchester Evening Star
March 5, 1951

Douglas School closed its basketball season last Friday night playing Rockville. High point scorers were June Gaskins and Barbara Turner. Though the boys did not win their game, Edward Curry, high point scorer, racked up 10 points.

Winchester Evening Star
March 23, 1951

The Douglas High School griders will play Carver Vocational in a homecoming game tomorrow afternoon at the Douglas Field beginning at 2:30 p.m. The game will be preceded by a parade at 1:30 p.m. starting at the Elks Home on Kent Street, to Piccadilly, West on Piccadilly to Main, south on Main to Cork, east on Cork to Kent, going north on Kent to the Douglas School.

Winchester Evening Star
November 15, 1951

The Douglas High School football team posted a 38-34 triumph over Carver High of Cumberland, Maryland Friday afternoon on the Douglas gridiron in the final game of the season. This victory was their eighth of this year against one defeat, that coming from the hands of Page Jackson of Charles Town, West Virginia by the score of 27-6. Douglas later defeated Charles Town by a 15-7 count. They hold twin victories over George Washington Carver, Manassas Regional High and Carver High. Their other lone win was a 34-0 verdict over Andrew Jackson. The outstanding players for the Douglas eleven were Charles Jackson and Eugene Watkins, speedy backs who have given the opposition much trouble all year.

Winchester Evening Star
November 20, 1951

Douglas High School 1963-1964 basketball team. Kneeling, left to right: William Beamer, Randolph Martin, Irvin Baltimore, Norman Blowe; standing, (left to right): Edwin K. Barksdale (coach), Herman Grimes, Clarence Curry. (555-77f)

Douglas High School girls' basketball team 1953-54. Sitting left to right: Marlene Johnson, Janet Lewis, Beverly Long, Audrey Curry, Edith Stern; standing, left to right: Shirley Bartlett, Jean Carol Finley, Sylvia Stephenson, Barbara Turner, Maggie Burks, Zita Laws, Grace Evans. (555-138)

The Douglas basketball team was host to the Howard High School basketball team from Piedmont, West Virginia, on Tuesday. The battle between the teams was terrific. Howard was victorious 58 to 23.

Winchester Evening Star
February 16, 1952

———————————

The basketball season is gradually coming to an end with some victories and some failures. Both boys' and girls' teams have shown great improvement this year.

Winchester Evening Star
March 9, 1952

———————————

The Douglas High School basketball team played its last game Thursday night with Andrew Jackson School from Luray. Douglas won by a score of 36-34. The game was sponsored by the Senior Class. The team has a rating of 3rd Place in the Tri-State League and will play in the tournament March 27, 28 and 29th in Martinsburg, West Virginia The eight top rating players will represent the school, playing the first game Thursday against Ramer High of Martinsburg. Much credit must be given to the coach, Mr. Hite, for the team's progress and success this year.

Winchester Evening Star
March 22, 1952

———————————

In a great comeback, the Douglas High School football team came from behind in the second half to tie Page Jackson of Charles Town 13-13, after giving up two first half touchdowns to the visitors in the Rouss Park game of last Thursday. Despite losing their entire squad to the Armed Forces, the Douglas team continues unbeaten having won over Luray's Andrew Jackson High School 12-6 in the season opener.

Winchester Evening Star
October 14, 1952

The Douglas School will hold its annual Homecoming tomorrow with the main feature of the day being a football game with Luray at the City Park on Route 50. At 1 p.m. the annual Homecoming parade will be held forming at the school and going south on Kent to Baker, west on Baker to Loudoun, south on Loudoun to Cork, east on Cork to Kent and north on Kent back to the school.

Winchester Evening Star
November 5, 1952

———————————

The Douglas High School girls and boys basketball teams will play a twin bill in the Douglas gym tomorrow night against Luray High School starting at 7:30 p.m. The girls who have lost a couple of one pointers while making a record of two wins, three losses and a tie will be trying to hit the 500 mark for the season. The boys will have the same problem, as they have won four while losing five.

Winchester Evening Star
March 4, 1953

———————————

The Douglas High School boys and girls basketball teams split a doubleheader with Luray Thursday night at the Douglas gym as the girls won by 24–12 score led by Audrey Curry and the boys lost 39–54. In the boys game the high men for Douglas were Michael Ford and Hubert Stephenson.

Winchester Evening Star
March 7, 1953

———————————

In two games this season, the Bulldogs are undefeated and unscored. On Saturday, they defeated Culpeper 6-0 as a blocked punt by Floyd Walker set up the lone touchdown. The first win for Douglas was a 47-0 win over Luray.

Winchester Evening Star
October 12, 1953

The Douglas High School girls basketball team will play the Johnson Williams girls team of Berryville in an exhibition game on Wednesday night at 7:30 o'clock at the Douglas Gymnasium.

Winchester Evening Star
October 27, 1953

———————————

Coach Edwin K. Barksdale, of the Douglas High School has an enviable position among the members of his profession. First: his team went through a six game season undefeated and untied and only allowed six points and second he will have the entire squad back for next season with the exception of an end. So there it is, a coach with a dream team - not a graduate on the list. Needless to say the Bulldogs took first place honors in the Tri-State League and next year they have hopes of increasing their schedule to include two or three more teams of first rate caliber. In going undefeated and untied, the Bulldogs spread their scoring among eleven men showing their well rounded attack. High man was Beverly Gaskins with five touchdowns and an extra point for 31 points. The rest in order were: Perry Dyer, 21; David Clinton, 20; Hubert Stephenson, 13; Floyd Walker, 12; Floyd Burks, 13; David Burks,12; John Carter, 8; James Prather, 6; Garland Williams, 6; and James Carter, 1. In addition to the players listed as scorers, the rest of the first and second team members are: Walter Payton, James Stephenson, Dabney Stephenson, Floyd Walker, Michael Ford, Robert Gaither, Morris Carter, Charles Grimes, Lawrence Curry, James Nelson, Alexander Thomas and Kenneth Carey as the manager.

Winchester Evening Star
December 7, 1953

Members of the Douglas High School Girls Basketball Team circa 1953-54. Left to right: Shirley Bartlett, Marlene Johnson, Barbara Turner. (555-139)

Douglas High School 1958 girls' basketball team. Left to right: Frances Washington, Dorothy Gant, Brenda Bundy, Joy Ann Gaskins, Anna Strother, Judith Gaither, Harriet Washington. (555-76)

The Douglas Bulldogs will wind up their basketball season tomorrow night at the Douglas Gym with a game against the Shenandoah All Stars, a collection of high school, college and independent players. In an opening game, the undefeated girls of Douglas will play the Harpers Ferry girls at 8:00 p.m. Tomorrow night will be the last night of the girl's season as well, although they have played only two games.

Winchester Evening Star
March 10, 1954

The first meeting for the Douglas High School football candidates has been called for tonight at 5:30 p.m. by Coach Edwin Barksdale. Practice sessions will open tomorrow afternoon at 5:30 p.m. and be the same time daily until school opens on September 7. Coach Barksdale has no idea of doing as well this season even though he has lost only two lettermen from that squad. Both of them, Perry Dyer and Jack Christian are both in the U.S. Army. With them went the height that Coach Barksdale's passers were hitting last year, but he has every other position served up as tight as any coach could hope for. The team will work out of some new Split-T formation plays which Coach Barksdale studied this summer under Jim Tatum of Maryland and Sal Hall of Virginia State College in special courses. Coach Barksdale is working on obtaining bleachers this season to prevent the crowding that has existed along the sidelines.

Winchester Evening Star
August 23, 1954

Douglas High's hopes of a second undefeated season in a row went down the hatch yesterday afternoon as it absorbed a home field 6-0 lost at the hands of powerful Cardozo High of Washington, D.C.

Winchester Evening Star
September 25, 1954

Douglas opened the Tri-State League football season yesterday with a splash running over Page Jackson of Charles Town 34-0 in a show of power that promises to earn the championship for the second straight year.

Winchester Evening Star
October 1, 1954

After an opening game 6-0 loss to Cardozo, the Douglas bulldogs have come along with a show of power in winning two straight by top heavy margins. Last night the Winchester school defeated Carver High of Rockville, Maryland 27-0 on the loser's home field. It was the first time that Douglas had played under lights in three seasons and it was the first time in many games that the lads had faced a single wing attack.

Winchester Evening Star
October 14, 1954

Douglas High hopes to run its current winning streak to three this Thursday afternoon when William C. Taylor High comes in for a 2 o'clock game. The Bulldogs will have to get past the best aerial attack they have faced yet. Coach E. K. Barksdale expressed the opinion that this week's game could easily be the toughest of the season not counting our opener against Cardozo.

Winchester Evening Star
October 19, 1954

The Douglas Bulldogs, playing in short spurts, managed to sustain three drives yesterday afternoon to defeat a green William Taylor High 18-0 on the local's field. It was the opening game this season for the Warrenton eleven and the fourth for Douglas.

Winchester Evening Star
October 22, 1954

Douglas romped to its fifth straight win of the season yesterday afternoon at Charles Town downing Page-Jackson 20-0 on a wet clay field.

Winchester Evening Star
November 6, 1954

Douglas High School vaunted Bulldogs will be shooting for their seventh straight win of the season at 2 p.m. tomorrow against Douglass of Leesburg, a school over which they already own a 23-0 win. The biggest fault with overconfidence against them has been the pass defense. It cost the Bulldogs a touchdown in the 40-6 win over Carver and it meant considerable yardage in other games. Last week when the Bulldogs trounced Douglas on its home field in Leesburg, it was homecoming for the Loudoun County School but the Winchester Douglas didn't have much sympathy for the occasion.

Winchester Evening Star
November 18, 1954

Douglas wound up a spectacular football season yesterday afternoon in fitting fashion as it walloped an outmanned Leesburg Douglass 45-0 in rain, fog and mud. Rebecca Robinson was crowned Homecoming Queen at halftime of the game. Although the pageantry was held during a pouring rain, it was a big success. The Gibson Drum and Bugle Corps took part in the half time ceremonies.

Winchester Evening Star
November 20, 1954

The first Douglas High School football team, 1945. Team members in uniform, identified by last name only. Front row, left to right: Carter, Williams, Brown, Festus, Burns, Finley; back row: Gaither, Thompson, Burks, Bartlett. In the right rear is Francis M. Jackson (teacher.) The purchase of the uniforms was sponsored by Bell Clothes Shop. (555-85)

1947 Brown Bombers football team made up of area players. Kneeling left to right: Moses Brown (water boy), Fred Taper, Clarence Good, F. Walker, Paul Johnson, Charles Lewis, John Cook, William "Billy" Grimes, Charles H. Myers, Harry C. Baylor. Standing, left to right: William Brown Sr. (booking agent), Spottswood Brown (manager), J.D. Warren, George Cary, L. Harris, Frank V. Day, James Hogans, George Cook, J. Tibbs, William Honesty, Herman Jackson Jr, P. Smith, Chester Jackson, Lee Honesty, George Hogans, Jasper L. Long, Boyd Cook, Thurston Clevenger (coach). (204-3)

Douglas High opens its basketball season tomorrow night with a home game against Andrew Jackson High of Luray. The varsity will get underway immediately following a girls game at 8 o'clock. The Bulldogs have two starting fives with an 11th man who can work in with each unit. He is Dabney Stephenson, fourth high man from last season. The first starting five for Coach Edwin Barksdale will be James Prather, Bob Burks, John Carter, Hubert Stephenson and Beverly Gaskins. The game will mark Douglas' first time in the Group III, Division Virginia Interscholastic Association, the other members of which are Harrisonburg and Berryville.

Winchester Evening Star
December 15, 1954

The Douglas High two-platoon basketball system paid off in big dividends last night on the home court as the Bulldogs slaughtered Andrew Jackson of Luray 92-5. The Luray team is coached by Kirk N. Gaskins Jr., son of the Douglas principal. No member of the Douglas squad was charged with more than one foul in the cleanly fought game. In the opening game last night, the Douglas' girls defeated the Luray girls 35-10.

Winchester Evening Star
December 17, 1954

The combined Douglas High and Douglas Alumni basketball teams will play an exhibition game against Shepherdstown's All Stars tonight in the Winchester school's gym. A preliminary game between two junior varsity groups will get underway this evening at 8 o'clock.

Winchester Evening Star
January 6, 1955

The Douglas High basketball team defeated the Shepherdstown All Stars last night 47-30 at the Winchester school's gym. Prather and Gaskins had eight a piece for the winners. In a preliminary game, the Douglas Whites took a 26-16 decision over the Douglas Blues. Lawrence Curry had 10 for the winners as did Tommy Washington for the losers.

Winchester Evening Star
January 7, 1955

Douglas ran into its toughest competition so far last night as Harrisonburg held the Bulldogs 56-37 win in a Tri-State League match. Top scorers for Douglas were Carter with 13, Prather with 12 and Robert Burks with 10. In a thrilling opener, the Douglas girls lost 31-28. Janet Lewis had 14 for the Bulldogs.

Winchester Evening Star
January 14, 1955

Douglas won its fourth straight game of the season last night with a 50-39 score over Carver High of Rockville on the Marylander's court. Starting with a rush, the Bulldogs piled up an early 17 point lead and then coasted home. Leading scorer for the Bulldogs was Carter with 20, Hubert Stephenson and Robert Burks with 11.

Winchester Evening Star
January 15, 1955

Douglas lost its first athletic event since September 24, last night dropping a 77-70 count to a powerful Lincoln High at Frederick, Maryland. The game which broke wide open in the second and third quarters reached its worst point for the Bulldogs going into the fourth when they held a 25 point deficit. By the four minute warning buzzer, they had shortened that gap to 8 points. Double figure players for Douglas were Robert Burks with 21, John Carter with 13 and Dabney Stephenson with 10. In the first game last night, Douglas JV won 35-32 in a battle right down to the wire.

Winchester Evening Star
January 19, 1955

Douglas High trimmed Page Jackson (52-31) in a twin basketball bill last night on the Winchester quintet's court but the JV's had to scrape down for their win. Using his two-platoon system right down the line, Coach Edwin Barksdale, had just one man, Carter with 10, in the two figure column. The Bulldogs have a season of five wins and one loss and have kept the opposition below the 40 mark in all but the 60-77 defeat by Lincoln.

Winchester Evening Star
January 21, 1955

Douglas was upset by Ramer High of Martinsburg 47-39 last night on the West Virginia's court as both teams found the range difficult. It was the first time the Bulldogs had been held under 40 points and only the second time an opponent had gone over that mark. High scorers for the Douglas team were Robert Burks - 14, John Carter - 11, and Stephenson - 10.

Winchester Evening Star
January 26, 1955

In a below par exhibition, the Douglas Bulldogs dropped a 56-52 count to Simms High at Harrisonburg last night to fall into a tie with their hosts for the lead in the Virginia Interscholastic Association. The teams share 2-1 records. The two players from Douglas in double figures were John Carter - 21, and James Prather - 12.

Winchester Evening Star
February 5, 1955

The Douglas Bulldogs won a twin bill last night at the expense of Leesburg's Douglass, the varsity taking the nightcap 58-53, after the JV took the opener 36-29. In the main game, John Carter, big gun of the Bulldogs all season, came through with 17 points. This time he had important help from Robert Burks who connected for 19 points. Leading the JVs to the opening game win was Kenneth Burks with 12 points and Walter Payton with 11.

Winchester Evening Star
February 9, 1955

Douglas High School football squad in action. c. 1949. (555-93)

Douglas School Bulldogs appliqué. From a display of Douglas School memorabilia, 2003. (555-124)

1949 Douglas High School football team and Homecoming Court during Homecoming. Front row, left to right: Charles Curry, Edward Curry, Albert Grimes, James Walden, Beverly Christian, Dunbar Spencer; second row, left to right: Roy Rhodes, William Watkins, Charles Jackson, Charles Burks, Celesta Carter, Charles Cook, Franklin Day; third row, left to right (women): Shirley Bartlett, Fitzhugh Christian (Homecoming Queen), Rosalie Bartlett, Ann Ford fourth row, left to right: Douglas Burns, Henry Bartlett, Harry Brown, Robert Cook, Charles Boles, Kenny Burks. (618-3)

Lincoln High of Frederick made it a clean sweep for the season over Douglas last night on the Bulldog's home court with a 55-38 score. High scorer for Douglas was John Carter with 20, and Robert Burks with 9. In the preliminary game, the Douglas girls lost a heart breaker 33-32 in the closing moments of play. Janet Lewis had 15 for Douglas and Audrey Curry had 10.

Winchester Evening Star
February 11, 1955

Douglas swept its season against Leesburg's Douglass last night with a convincing 63-41 win on the Winchester five's court. Opening up a 19-6 magin at the end of the first quarter, the Bulldogs pulled steadily away behind the sharpshooting of John Carter who rang up 30 points. This was the high mark for the Winchester club this season topping Carter's own record of 21 points which he shared with Robert Burks.

Winchester Evening Star
February 16, 1955

An experienced Douglas quintet had little trouble with Johnson Williams of Berryville last night winning 71-28 on the loser's court. Leading the assault on the Johnson Williams basket was John Carter, ace of the Bulldogs, with 26 points. Hubert Stephenson and Beverly Gaskins each had 10 points for the Bulldogs. With this win the Bulldogs jumped to a season record of nine and four as they defeated Page Jackson of Charlestown, 68-61 on Friday night. In that game, the top man for Douglas was the same John Carter with a 26 point performance.

Winchester Evening Star
February 22, 1955

Minus their coach and definitely down on their shooting, the Douglas Bulldogs dropped a 78-52 game to North Street High of Hagerstown last night. Even with the direction of Coach Edwin Barksdale, in bed because of an abscess, it is doubtful if the Bulldogs could have stopped the red hot Marylanders last night. John Carter had to settle for second place last night among the Bulldog scorers as his 14 points was three under the performance of Hubert Stephenson.

Winchester Evening Star
February 23, 1955

Douglas upped its Tri-State League stock a long ways last night with a doubleheader win over Luray and Martinsburg. In the opener, the host Bulldogs walloped Andrew Jackson of Luray 48-10, and then they surprised Ramer of Martinsburg 87-19. Two factors combined to make the main game a rout. John Carter was really red hot, racking up 19 field goals and 8 free throws for 46 points. The game was finally called in the last quarter with just three visitors left on the court after fouls had taken their toll. They brought an eight man squad and five fouled out, one of their top stars in the first quarter.

Winchester Evening Star
February 25, 1955

Douglas ran into a little more competition than it might have expected last night and had trouble defeating Johnson Williams 56-45. John Carter who went wild last week with a 46 point performance against Ramer of Martinsburg was held to eight points. James Prather was high man in this one with 13 points.

Winchester Evening Star
March 1, 1955

North Street High of Hagerstown, Maryland defeated Douglas 66-61 last night on the victor's court to sweep its two game series. Hubert Stephenson of the Bulldogs was the lone man in the 20s. Robert Burks was next with 15 and John Carter had to settle for a 12 point third place.

Winchester Evening Star
March 9, 1955

The Douglas Bulldogs leave for the Virginia Interscholastic Association Basketball Tournament tomorrow morning with an excellent chance of returning to Winchester with the 1st place trophy. Played at Harrisonburg, the tournament will be composed of four teams: Berryville, Harrisonburg, Luray and Winchester. Ten men will make the trip with Coach Edwin Barksdale and Douglas Custodian, Roy Denny. They are Dabney Stephenson, Robert Burks, John Carter, Michael Ford, Hubert Stephenson, James Prather, Floyd Burks, Beverly Gaskins, Walter Payton, and Arthur Lewis Jr.

Winchester Evening Star
March 4, 1955

In a one day basketball tournament at Harrisonburg Saturday, Douglas High captured the Virginia Interscholastic Association crown for District 3, Group III. The Bulldogs won their semi-final opener 102-9 over Luray's Andrew Jackson and then took the final 50-39 from Harrisonburg's Lucy Simms. With the handsome gold trophy and title, the Bulldogs now have the right to represent the district in the Group III State Championship at Virginia State College on March 11 and 12.

Winchester Evening Star
March 7, 1955

Disappointment hit the Douglas Bulldogs early in their quest for state honors in Group III basketball last night at Petersburg. It came in the form of a 49-40 defeat at the hands of Pocahontas of Powhatan and ended the Winchester school's expected three day trip all too soon.

Winchester Evening Star
March 12, 1955

Douglas High School Bulldogs 1950 football team. Kneeling, left to right: Wesley Jackson, Charles H. Jackson, Eugene Watkins, Leon Boles, Edward Curry, Louis Johnson, Charles Boles, Alphonse Jordan; standing, left to right: Hubert Stephenson, Basil Puller, Nimrod Turner, Franklin Day, Beverly Christian, William Watkins, James Waldon, Charles Dendy (coach). (555-94)

Douglas High School football team. Photo taken in front of school, c. 1951. Kneeling, left to right: Lathan Williams, Charles Boles, James Prather, Leon Boles, Wesley Jackson, Charles Jackson, Eugene Watkins, Hubert Stephenson, Edward Curry, Nimrod Turner, John Carter; standing, left to right: Charles Dendy (coach), Franklin Day, Basil Puller, Thomas Gaither, Kenneth Cook, Floyd Burks, Michael Ford, Walter Peyton, David Clinton, Beverly Christian, William Watkins, William Nash (assistant coach). (555-92)

The Tri-State Colored Basketball Tournament opened at the National Guard Armory last night with two top flight games, a ballet performance and promise of a rousing time tonight and tomorrow night. In last night's quarterfinal round, Ramer High of Martinsburg was eliminated 74-56 by Howard High of Piedmont and Douglass High of Leesburg was dropped 72-62 by the host Douglas quint of Winchester. At one point in the final quarter, the host led by 30 points but Coach Barksdale substituted then and the margin dropped. Three Douglas players reached double figures: Robert Burks - 26, John Carter - 17, and Dabney Stephenson 12.

Winchester Evening Star
March 18, 1955

In the consolation game opening the evening's doubleheader, Lincoln High of Frederick took third place with an 82-65 victory over the host quintet Douglas High of Winchester. The Bulldogs were without the service of their key man, John Carter, who played the first two games with a broken finger, had a cast up to his elbow for the final game and never left the bench. Robert Burks was a unanimous choice to the tournament 1st team All Stars, and Dabney Stephenson was named to the second team.

Winchester Evening Star
March 21, 1955

Douglas High opened its football season at home yesterday on a sad note, dropping a 14-0 decision to triple decked Cardozo High of Washington, DC. Although the Bulldogs lost this opening game, there is good reason to figure they will go along the rest of the way with no blots on their record – the same way they did in 1954 after dropping the opener to Cardozo 6-0.

Winchester Evening Star
September 21, 1955

The Douglas Bulldogs are going to have their hands full this Friday as they play host to the 1954 Virginia Group III Champs of Watson High of Covington in a 2:00 p.m. game. The Bulldogs have a season record of 1-1, the loss being a 14-0 decision to Cardozo High of Washington, D.C. and the win being an identical score over Carver High of Rockville, Maryland. Douglas has dropped only two games in three seasons and they were both to Cardozo.

Winchester Evening Star
October 12, 1955

Douglas began gathering momentum for its late season drive yesterday afternoon by ramming a 6-0 defeat down the throats of the Virginia Group III champions of Watson High of Covington. The victory was the second straight for the Bulldogs.

Winchester Evening Star
October 15, 1955

An intercepted pass was the deciding factor yesterday afternoon as the Douglas High bulldogs, the sharpness of their play perhaps smoothed off a bit by over confidence, went down 6-0 before Charlestown at the legion field there.

Winchester Evening Star
October. 22, 1955

A touchdown in the last five seconds of play gave a powerful Leesburg eleven the long end of a 12-6 score over the Douglas Bulldogs here yesterday afternoon.

Winchester Evening Star
October 29, 1955

Douglas climbed back into the win column yesterday afternoon for the first time in three weeks with a 19-14 victory of Carver High of Rockville, Maryland. But the Bulldogs had to do it the hard way with a 14-0 score staring them in the face as they left the field at halftime. The TDs were made by Garland Williams from the five yard line, from Lawrence Curry from the six and from Alexander Thomas from the five. The one extra point was made by Williams.

Winchester Evening Star
November 5, 1955

Douglas ends season with 29-6 victory over Warrenton. Jean Carol Finley was crowned Homecoming Queen during halftime ceremonies.

Winchester Evening Star
November 18, 1955

Behind 19-14 at the half, Manassas' tall quint roared home fast for a seven point victory over the Douglas Bulldogs last night 45-38 on the Manassas court. Double figure men for the Bulldogs were John Carter - 15 and Beverly Gaskins - 13.

Winchester Evening Star
December 14, 1955

After losing its opening game to Manassas 45-38 on Tuesday, the Douglas quint came back on its home court last night to do what it promised – whip the same club. It accompanied the reversal of form to the tune of 41-33, giving the Bulldogs a one point edge after the split. The top men of the Bulldogs, John Carter and Beverly Gaskins lived up to advance publicity by scoring 18 points apiece for high honors to the delight of most of the 165 fans present.

Winchester Evening Star
December 16, 1955

Douglas High School 1953 Bulldogs football team. Front row, left to right: Robert Gaither, Beverly Gaskins, David Burks, John Carter, Hubert Stephenson, Michael Ford, James Stephenson, Perry Dyer, Walter Peyton; second row, left to right: Kenneth Cary (manager), Lawrence Curry, Floyd Walker, Morris Carter, James Carter, Floyd Burks, James Prather, Edwin K. Barksdale (coach), Dabney Stephenson, Charles Grimes, David Clinton, James Nelson, Garland Williams, Alexander Thomas. (555-90a)

Douglas High School Bulldogs football team suited up to play in 1955. Front row, left to right: Ronald Washington (manager), James Carter, Charles Walker (manager), Lawrence Curry, Frank Lavender, Benjamin Brown (manager), Thomas Washington (statistician); second row, left to right: David Clinton (captain), Floyd Burks (co-captain), Louis Newman, Lamont Johnson, Allen Corley, Robert Gaither, Kenneth Cary, James Nelson, coach Edwin K. Barksdale; third row, left to right: Shepherd Harris, John Shields, James Stephenson, Kenneth Burks, Charles Grimes, Garland Williams; fourth row, left to right: Charles Corley, William Tigney, Charles Harris, John Spencer, Charles Boles, Stephen Newman. (555-96)

Douglas High opens its 1956 part of the basketball season tomorrow night with the first of a two-game series with the Luray quint – both games being scheduled for the Bulldogs' court as Luray's court isn't ready. Tonight's activities begin with a girl's game at 7:30 o'clock.

Winchester Evening Star
January 4, 1956

Scoring at will with the first team on the floor for just two periods, the Douglas Bulldogs tarnished an inexperienced Luray quint 83-17 last night. Douglas had five men in double figures, John Carter 23, Beverly Gaskins 13, Floyd Burks 11, and Robert Gaither and Lawrence Curry both with 10.

Winchester Evening Star
January 6, 1956

A last quarter rally by Martinsburg's Ramer High was enough to stop Douglas 50-41 last night on the West Virginian's court. It was a bitter pill for the Bulldogs after leading 39-34 with three and a half minutes left in the game. Only two Douglas men reached double figures, Beverly Gaskins and Floyd Burks both with eleven. The host team put two men on Carter and they held him to two points.

Winchester Evening Star
January 7, 1956

On January 17, the Douglas High School played the Page-Jackson High School of Charles Town, West Virginia on the West Virginian's home court. The Douglas varsity won 52-45 but the JV lost.

Winchester Evening Star
January 21, 1956

After a close first half at Douglas last night, the host Bulldogs, poured it on Leesburg's Douglass to the tune of 68-43 for their fifth win in seven starts. Pacing the Bulldogs attack was: Robert Gaither, with 11 points, John Carter with 22 points and Beverly Gaskins with 20.

Winchester Evening Star
January 27, 1956

The Douglas varsity had an easy time of it last night surprising a strong Page-Jackson of Charles Town by a 56-34 count but the JV's had to pull their 26-25 win out of the fire in the last second of play. Douglas varsity had four men in double figures: John Carter - 15, Beverly Gaskins and James Stephenson - 12, and Robert Gaither - 11.

Winchester Evening Star
February 3, 1956

A charging Lucy Simms quint turned back the hustling Douglas Bulldogs at Harrisonburg last night forging ahead in the second half to win 68-49. John Carter contributed 22 and Beverly Gaskins 16 for the Bulldogs.

Winchester Evening Star
February 4, 1956

Douglas found the error of its ways in trying a man for man against Johnson Williams last night in time to trip the host Berryville quint by a 58-42 score. Double figure men for the Bulldogs were: Beverly Gaskins - 20 and John Carter 19.

Winchester Evening Star
February 10, 1956

Shooting at a 44 percent clip, Douglas bounced out a three game slump last night at Berryville to trim Johnson Williams 86-66. The Winchester school's record is now 9-4. John Carter scored 25 while John Spencer scored 18. Ninth graders Lee Mason turned in 12 points and James Walker turned in 16.

Winchester Evening Star
February 16, 1956

Leesburg's Douglass surprised Winchester's Douglas last night by a 62-54 count at Leesburg after losing by 25 points in their other meeting.

Winchester Evening Star
February 11, 1956

In defeating Lucy Simms of Harrisonburg 65-51 last night at Douglas, the Bulldogs reversed an earlier loss 68-49 on the Rockingham County quint's court and stepped into the Group III Tournament picture. Lucy Simms Principal Austin Stitt and Coach William W. Perry issued a joint statement to the *Winchester Evening Star* this morning that their team would not be able to play the rubber game for the district title with Douglas because of other commitments tonight and tomorrow and were conceding to the Bulldogs. The schools are deadlocked at 5-1. Three Douglas men in double figures were: John Carter - 20, James Stephensson - 15 and Floyd Burks - 10.

Winchester Evening Star
February. 24, 1956

It took two overtime periods for Ramer High of Martinsburg to turn the trick on Douglas last night 48-47. High point men for Douglas were John Carter - 17 and Robert Gaither - 13.

Winchester Evening Star
February 28, 1966

Douglas High School 1955 football team. Seated, left to right: Thomas Washington (statistician), and Charles Walker (manager); kneeling; front row kneeling, left to right: David Clinton, Charles Grimes, James Nelson, William Tigney, Lawrence Curry, William Dyer, Charles Corley, James Carter; second row standing, left to right: John B. Cook (assistant coach), Kenneth Cary, William Shepherd Harris, John Spencer, Charles Boles, Robert Gaither, Harold Scott, John R. Carter, Edwin K. Barksdale (coach); top row: John Shields, James Stephenson, Garland Williams, Floyd Burks, Kenneth Burks, Allen Corley, Charles E. Harris, Lamont Johnson. (555-86)

Douglas High School 1957-1958 football team. Front row, left to right: Ronald Moten, Shepherd Harris Jr., Raymond Blowe Jr., Webster Washington Jr, Jerome Jackson, Stephen Newman, James Elwood Walker; Second row, left to right: Garland Williams, Kenneth Burks, James Nelson, Clifford Lee Mason, Frank Lavender, Randolph Carter, John Spencer, Edwin K. Barksdale (coach). (555-154)

Douglas 101

The Invitational Field Day will be held May 5, starting at 1 p.m. at Douglas High School. Schools from the surrounding cities of Berryville, Martinsburg, Rockville, Luray, Warrenton, Charles Town, Hagerstown and Frederick have been invited. The events in which these schools will participate are dodge ball, dashes, jumping, volley ball and softball. Following the field day events, a social dance will be held sponsored by the senior class.

Winchester Evening Star
May 1, 1956

The first meeting for the 1956 Douglas High football candidates will be held tomorrow at 5:30 p.m. at the school. Coach Barksdale, who has had winning seasons ever since joining the Douglas staff asked that all players bring pencils and notebook. First practice for the Bulldogs will be on Friday. Coach Barksdale will have a first rate assistant this year in John B. Cooke, telephone company employee.

Winchester Evening Star
August 29, 1956

The Douglas Bulldogs open their 1956 football season on Friday afternoon against the toughest foe they'll meet this year, Cardozo High. The Washington, D.C. School is host for this one, the first time in three meetings. Both games have been thrillers, Cardozo winning 6-0 in 1954 and 14-0 in 1955. These scores are more significant when it's pointed out that the big Washington school has an enrollment in its senior class far greater than the entire Douglas enrollment.

Winchester Evening Star
September 18, 1956

When Douglas and Page-Jackson schedule a football game they intend to play it regardless. That's exactly what happened yesterday afternoon on the Bulldog's home field despite a driving rain which started early in the day and didn't

quit. The West Virginians turned out to be better mudders, eventually wining 4-0 on a pair of safeties.

Winchester Evening Star
September 26, 1956

When trouble comes, it lands in bunches. Already owning two loses, the Bulldogs had hoped to get back on the win trail against the Covington eleven. Coach Barksdale had to field a team that was minus his ace quarterback, John Carter, James Stephenson, Charles Corley, Allen Corley, Kenneth Burks, Lawrence Curry and John Spencer all 1st string players.

Winchester Evening Star
October. 13, 1956

Behind the quarterbacking of John Carter and the running of Lawrence Curry, the Douglas Bulldogs ran over visiting Carver High of Rockville, Maryland yesterday 32-0.

Winchester Evening Star
October 20, 1956

Douglass Leesburg lives up to three touchdowns boast by trouncing Douglas Winchester 19-0.

Winchester Evening Star
October 27, 1956

Douglas High will play host to Carver of Culpeper here tomorrow in the Bulldogs annual Homecoming. A high point of tomorrow's Homecoming events will be the crowning of Jacqueline Williams, an eighth grader as Homecoming Queen. Members of her court are Arlene Blowe, Margaret Jackson, Joy Ann Gaskins and Janice Williams.

Winchester Evening Star
October 31, 1956

The Douglas Bulldogs bounced back in the fourth quarter yesterday to overcome a one point deficit and beat Carver of Culpepper 12-7 in the rain and mud.

Winchester Evening Star
November 2, 1956

The Douglas Bulldogs open their basketball season tomorrow night with a home doubleheader against Luray's Andrew Jackson High. A girl's game will start the evening. This year's team could be the most interesting produced at Douglas.

Winchester Evening Star
December 5, 1956

Douglas wins first game 56-7 over Andrew Jackson of Luray. The Douglas girls won their game 18-12. John Carter was top scorer for the men and Margaret Jackson was high scorer for the ladies.

Winchester Evening Star
December 7, 1956

Douglas won its sixth game of the season last night against just two losses as it downed host Ramer of Martinsburg 58-35. John Carter scored 29 and Benny Brown 10.

Winchester Evening Star
January 26, 1957

Douglas Bulldogs jump season's record to 7-2 with a 54-49 win over Carver. Lee Mason topped John Carter with 16, Carter had 14 and Benny Brown contributed 10.

Winchester Evening Star
January 30, 1957

Douglas High School 1956 Bulldogs football team. Front row, left to right: Kenneth Cary, John Spencer, Charles Corley, Allan Corley, James Stephenson, Shepherd Harris, Harold Scott; second row, left to right: Kenneth Burks, James Carter, John Carter, Garland Williams. (555-91)

Douglas High School 1959 Bulldogs football team, unbeaten and untied. Front row, left to right: Michael Gilkerson, Richard L. Harris, John Alsberry, Stanley Long, Paul S. Walker; second row), left to right: Noah A. Laws, Robert Cooper, Herman Grimes, Lawrence E. Carter, Melvin Cooper, Ronald V. Moten, Frank Lavender; third row, left to right: Theodore Tolliver, Charles B. Harris, Herman Washington, Bushrod S. Harris, Joseph Jackson, Clarence Curry, Charles Corley, Edwin K. Barksdale (coach). (555-87)

Douglas won its fourth game in a row and eight out of ten for the season last night as it dumped visiting Ramer of Martinsburg 53-34. John Carter contributed 17 and James Walker 10 for the Bulldogs.

Winchester Evening Star
February 1, 1957

Red hot Charles Rutherford, single handedly fought off a Douglas comeback last night at the Winchester school to give Page-Jackson a 62-69 win. John Carter scored 19 points, James Stephenson 18 and James Walker 11.

Winchester Evening Star
February 8, 1957

Luther Jackson of Fairfax showed its power last night by trimming host Douglas 44-45 before a crowd of better than 250 fans. James Stephenson was top scorer with 10 and Lee Mason 12. John Carter was held to 2 points.

Winchester Evening Star
February 13, 1957

Behind all the way in the final game of the Group III District 3 Basketball Tournament at the N.G. Armory Saturday night, Douglas came up with a last second basket to earn an overtime period. The victory qualified the Bulldogs for state competition but the site and dates of the tournament have not been decided yet. The season record for the Bulldogs so far (official games) is 12-4.

Winchester Evening Star
February 25, 1957

District 3 Champions Douglas is host to District 2 Champ, S. C. Abrams High of Fluvanna County, Saturday night in a quarter finals event. The winner goes to Virginia State College at Petersburg next Friday morning for the State Semi-Finals.

Winchester Evening Star
March 1, 1957

Douglas is on the way to the State's Group III Semi-Finals at Virginia State College next Friday thanks to a convincing win over District 2 Champion Abrams High 66-37. Lee Mason contributed 17, Benny Brown 16, and John Carter 10.

Winchester Evening Star
March 4, 1957

Douglas High basketballers left by car this morning for the long trip to Petersburg and the group III tournament. Douglas will meet St. Claire Walker.

Winchester Evening Star
March 8, 1957

Winchester Douglas' Bulldogs drops a thriller to Leesburg's Douglass 61-59. Leading the scorers for Douglas were Benny Brown 17, John Carter 16, Lee Mason 13, and James Walker 12.

Winchester Evening Star
March 13, 1957

Winchester's Douglas High pulled a rabbit out of the hat at Martinsburg last night defeating Leesburg's Douglass 51-41 after two regular season defeats. This win sends the Bulldogs into the Tri-State Tournament finals against Charles Town's Page Jackson. John Carter had 17 and Benny Brown 13 for the Bulldogs.

Winchester Evening Star
March 23, 1957

Page Jackson High of Charlestown won the Tri State Tournament by turning back Winchester's Douglas 50-39. James Walker had 12 points, Lee Mason 10, John Carter 5, and Benny Brown 4.

Winchester Evening Star
March 25, 1957

When Douglas High wound up its 1956-57 basketball season with a grand total of 1,205 points as compared to 989 by the opposition. The result was a 14-7 record, a district championship trophy and a runner up trophy for the Tri-State. Individually, John Carter was the outstanding scorer for Douglas as he has for two seasons. He sank 358 points for a 17 average. Others scorers were Lee Mason 207, James Stephenson 181, Jimmy Walker 142, Tommy Washington 121 and Benny Brown 103.

Winchester Evening Star
March 27, 1957

The football team journeyed to Warrenton last Friday only to experience a great disappointment. Due to a critical situation which existed, the boys returned with only the memory. A last quarter touchdown and a broken drive made the difference between winning and losing for Douglas yesterday afternoon. Douglass of Leesburg made with a 17-7 victory in the snazziest last quarter of many seasons here.

Winchester Evening Star
October 4, 1957

Winless Douglas spotted visiting Carver High of Rockville seven points yesterday afternoon and flashed ahead to a 22-7 victory. During halftime, 1956 queen, Jackie Williams, crowned this year's queen, Ann Ransom.

Winchester Evening Star
November 2, 1957

Douglas tramples Carver 19-0. After losing the first four games, the Bulldogs finished with a 2-4 record.

Winchester Evening Star
November 9, 1957

Douglas Bulldogs stall Johnson Williams' rally 58-53. In the preliminary game, the Douglas girls won 23-16. Margaret Jackson tossed in 13 points, Elaine Parks had 6 and Delores Dyer had 4.

Winchester Evening Star
December 13, 1957

Douglas High showed signs of opening up a wide gap against its opponents this season as it roamed all over Johnson Williams court last night in defeating the Berryville club 81-44. In the junior varsity game, Douglas won 34-18.

Winchester Evening Star
December 17, 1957

The Bulldogs have a pair of away games tonight and tomorrow before a long stretch to the January 30 home date with Page-Jackson. The Douglas varsity has dropped one game to Simms of Harrisonburg and the JV here is unbeaten. This year the Bulldogs have a fine chance of being the best in the school's history, particularly with an unbeaten junior varsity as well as an undefeated girl's team.

Winchester Evening Star
January 16, 1958

For the eighth time this season, Douglas stepped to the winner's circle last night defeating Andrew Jackson of Luray 90-40 here. Five Bulldogs reached double figures: James Walker - 18, Tommy Washington - 14, Benny Brown and Lee Mason both with 13 and Ronnie Moten with 10. The girls won their fourth in a row in an unbeaten season with Margaret Jackson leading with 17 points, Elaine Parks with 7 and Frances Washington with 2.

Winchester Evening Star
January 24, 1958

Douglas nips Page Jackson with balance 63-56. Ronnie Moten scored 22 points, James Walker had 18, and Lee Mason added 15 for the Bulldogs.

Winchester Evening Star
January 9, 1959

Douglas defeats Johnson Williams 63-46. High point men for the Bulldogs were Lee Mason with 21 and Ronnie Moten with 21.

Winchester Evening Star
January 23, 1959

Douglas raps Lucy Simms 57-48 and coasted home with a big Group III win. James Walker was high man with 19. Lee Mason contributed 13 and Ronnie Moten 12. Douglas now owns a 6-1 record.

Winchester Evening Star
January 24, 1959

Douglass defeats Douglas 72-42. The Douglas Junior Varsity won their game 20-19 with James Brown scoring 9, and Eugene Washington 6.

Winchester Evening Star
January 27, 1959

Douglas pulls furious rally to win 58-53 over Page Jackson of Charles Town. James Walker scored 10 points in exactly one minute and 20 seconds to send Winchester home with the big seventh win. James Walker was high man for the bulldogs with 22 points, Ronnie Moten 16 and Lee Mason 12.

Winchester Evening Star
January 28, 1959

Douglas blocks Ramer shooters in 56-25 spree bringing their season record to 8-2. Nobody was real high for Douglas but Ronnie Moten -15, James Walker - 14, and Lee Mason -13 gave the host club balance. Last night, the Bulldogs pressed the visitors so hard all the way that they couldn't breathe. In the second quarter for example, the West Virginians were held to two free shots. From now on according to Coach Barksdale, the Bulldogs are going to press everyone, even if they go home dead tired and not showing many points.

Winchester Evening Star
January 30, 1959

Douglas wins 9th as Carver falters 65-61. Behind by 10 points going into the final period, the Bulldogs came up with a 20-6 margin to win going away. Again balance among the bulldog scorers: Ronnie Moten (18), James Walker (18) and Lee Mason (18.)

Winchester Evening Star
February 5, 1959

Douglas finished regular season with 12-2 record after upsetting Douglass Leesburg 57-53. Top scorer was James Walker - 17, George Curry 16, Lee Mason - 14. James Walker was far and away the night's star player as he and Ronnie Moten cleared the boards in the zone defense. In the preliminary game, the Douglas girls lost to the Douglass girls by four points.

Winchester Evening Star
February 20, 1959

Ronald Moten has 39 points in Douglas win over Watson High School of Covington, Va. 79-35. Lee Mason helped with 11, James Walker 9, George Curry and John Laws had 6 each. For the record hunters, Moten's performance was second highest in school history. Another Douglas sharpshooter, John Carter, had 51 against Ramer of Martinsburg.

Winchester Evening Star
March 6, 1959

Douglas trips Buckley-Lages 68-67. It was a thriller all the way but the stars were John Laws with his side shots and George Curry with his outside (20 footers). Laws and Curry both finished with 16, Ronnie Moten 14 and Lee Mason with 13.

Winchester Evening Star
March 11, 1959

Douglas was bounced from the State Group III Tournament 77-55 by Storemont's St Claire Walker. Lee Mason scored 19 points, George Curry 12, and Ronnie Moten 11.

Winchester Evening Star
March 14, 1959

Douglas Rallies Against Determined Simms – 34-0. That one half of play plus a sizzling halftime blast from Coach Barksdale was all it took to get the Bulldogs rolling in the second half. The TDs were by Noah Laws, John Laws, Lawrence Carter, Lee Mason and Ronnie Moten.

Winchester Evening Star
October 14, 1959

Unbeaten and untied Douglas took on strong Douglass of Leesburg here yesterday afternoon and proved that the record is no fluke. The Bulldogs won 21-0. Kenneth Cary, Noah Laws scored touchdowns. Lawrence Carter scored a touchdown and all three extra points.

Winchester Evening Star
October 31, 1959

The unbeaten Bulldogs will close out their season against Manassas. The Bulldogs have scored 109 points and have allowed only 7 by their opponents. This will be Homecoming and the queen will be crowned at halftime. A parade will begin at 1:30 pm and travel from the school on North Kent to the Elks Club, turn around and head north on Kent to Kern and move east to Fremont Street, north to Liberty Avenue, west to Kent and back to the school.

Winchester Evening Star
November 5, 1959

Douglas scored a double victory last night as its JV defeated Criser High's JV 64-20. Noah Laws scored 27, James Brown - 12 and Herman Washington added 12. Douglas varsity won 50-25. High scorers were Kenneth Pye with 21 points, Ronald Moten with 15.

Winchester Evening Star
December 9, 1959

Seven points behind with three and a half minutes to go, Douglas pulled one out of the fire last night on its home court against Lucy Simms of Harrisonburg, Va. winning 47-44. The Bulldogs scored 10 points in 3½ minutes. The Bulldogs were led by Ronnie Moten with 22 and John Laws with 13.

Winchester Evening Star
December 11, 1959

Unbeaten Douglas High turned on all its jets last night with an 86-47 home court victory over Johnson-Williams. Leading the scoring for Douglas was George Curry with 29, John Laws had 21 and Ronnie Moten had 19.

Winchester Evening Star
December 13, 1959

Bulldogs hold Appreciation Night Friday for new board. Hearing the school needed an electric scoreboard for basketball; a group of citizens promptly went to work a month ago and gathered in enough cash to install a $432.50 scorer at Douglas. Henry Lowry and Bill Battaile started the ball rolling for the scoreboard.

Winchester Evening Star
January 5, 1960

Douglas played to a standing room only crowd last night, as it rode to its fourth straight by the convincing margin of 71-27 over Criser of Front Royal.

Winchester Evening Star
January 9, 1960

Douglas Bulldogs performed like champions with a 67-61 win over host Johnson Williams of Berryville. Richard Johnson scored 24 points, Kenneth Pye 17 and George Curry 14.

Winchester Evening Star
January 13, 1960

Douglas spotted host Lucy Simms of Harrisonburg a two point margin in the first half and then roared to a 56-49 victory with a 56 percent goal effort in the final two quarters. The JV's won their game 66-31. Tops JV scorers were Richard Harris with 24 and Noah Laws with 22.

Winchester Evening Star
January 16, 1960

For the first time since school opened in September, a loss was tacked on the Douglas record for its boy's teams. After the football team went unbeaten and untied, the varsity and junior varsity basketball squads picked up the tempo. The Douglas Bulldogs were beaten by Page Jackson of Charles Town 52-45. The Douglas JV won 26-25.

Winchester Evening Star
January 30, 1960

A mob of Winchester fans turned out at Douglas last night to see if the Bulldogs could avenge their only defeat of the season and they left happy. The Douglas Bulldogs defeated Page Jackson of Charlestown 54-47. Top scorer for Douglas was Lee Mason with 16 points, John Laws and George Curry added 7 each. The Douglas JVs won their 7th straight 34-16.

Winchester Evening Star
February 3, 1960

Douglas ran its season record to 10-1 last night with a home court win over Ramer of Martinsburg. The West Virginians took a 54-39 licking thanks to the nimble hands of Bulldogs Ronald Moten who fired 30 points. It was the first game for Moten since he won the Sportsmanship Trophy given by the Sports Department of the WInchester Evening Star. Second place honors went to Noah Laws with 10 points.

Winchester Evening Star
February 20, 1960

An incident at Douglas High this week couldn't be better explained that in the words of television's Chester A. Riley who says, "What a revolting development." Rolling along undefeated in District 3 Group III basketball with the tournament set for tomorrow night, the Bulldogs suddenly found themselves minus their star player, 6-3 Ronald Moten. Because of a technicality, Moten has been declared ineligible and all of the games played by the Bulldogs in the league have been forfeited. Back in the eighth grade, Moten's name was put on the roster just in case the team needed him. He wasn't needed until the 10th grade but his name has been on the list for four years before this season and that's the limit in Virginia. The Bulldogs had been in first place in league competition with a 6-0 record but will now enter the tournament as the fourth place club with a 0-6 mark.

Winchester Evening Star
February 26, 1960

Johnson Williams of Berryville came home from the District 3 tournament losing to Lucy Simms of Harrisonburg, Virginia. The tournament MVP award went to George Curry of the Douglas Bulldogs who kept the Bulldogs in shooting range all the way, particularly in the final quarter when he made 17 points. Curry finished with 25 points.

Winchester Evening Star
February 29, 1960

Douglas romped to a 25-6 win over Page Jackson of Charles Town yesterday afternoon. Senior Lawrence Carter had a hand in the new look for the Bulldogs with a design for their helmets, while Tuscan Jasper's band added a lot to the occasion with a halftime overture. Next week, the Bulldogs play Johnson Williams of Berryville but it doesn't shape up much on paper because it's the first time that Berryville has tried football.

Winchester Evening Star
September 25, 1960

Douglas Bulldogs romp to fabulous 74-0 win of Johnson Williams of Berryville. After half of the first quarter was over, Coach Barksdale, jerked his first string lineup for the afternoon with a 20-0 lead.

Winchester Evening Star
October 1, 1960

Douglas scored on the third play from scrimmage yesterday afternoon at Harrisonburg and then watched the Lucy Simms defense fall apart under a steady bombardment as the Bulldogs swept to a 53-0 victory. On defense the Bulldogs were rugged, holding Harrisonburg to three first downs while rolling up 12 themselves.

Winchester Evening Star
October 8, 1960

Douglas shatters Douglass of Leesburg as five players score TDs. This win was the fourth in a row for Douglas and has a season total of 185 against 13. This is the highest scoring backfield in school history.

Winchester Evening Star
October 22, 1960

Douglas and Cardoza butted heads in a defensive duel for one half of their game here yesterday afternoon with the Bulldogs showing a 2-0 advantage at intermission. Then the dream bubble broke with a roar and Cardozo crashed its way to a 31-2 decision ending Douglas hopes of an unundefeated season and untied season in a most decisive manner.

Winchester Evening Star
Octoberr 29, 1960

Undiscouraged by last week's first loss of the season against Cardoza of Washington, Douglas bounced back under the lights last night to trounce host Jeanne Dean of Manassas 26-0.

Winchester Evening Star
November 5, 1960

Douglas Homecoming set for 2 pm Friday. They will host Lucy Simms of Harrisonburg. In their own class, Douglas gridders are potent. John Laws, George Curry, Lawrence Carter, Noah Laws, Eugene Polston (a guard)), Clarence Curry, Charles Harris, Stanley Long, Paul Walker, Charles Walker and Leroy Woodson have all scored TDs and most of them have scored several.

Winchester Evening Star
November 9, 1960

Douglas continued along its merry way yesterday afternoon, celebrating Homecoming by topping Lucy Simms of Harrisonburg 40-4. Yesterday's stars were the Laws brothers, John and Noah. Maxine Blowe was crowned Homecoming Queen by last year's queen, Dorothy Scott. This year's court included Betty Jo Payne, Sharon Williams, Katherine Ford and Linda Long.

Winchester Evening Star
November 12, 1960

Douglas closes its season with a 7-1 record defeating Johnson-Williams of Berryville 74-12. Noah Laws was the outstanding scorer for the season with at least one trip behind the goal line every time the Bulldogs played.

Winchester Evening Star
November 21, 1960

A last ditch stand by Douglas was just enough to stop Group I, Luther P. Jackson 45-44 yesterday on opening night for the Bulldogs.

Winchester Evening Star
December 3, 1960

After scoring 74 points twice this year against Johnson-Williams in football, Douglas dropped to 73 last night at Berryville in a winning basketball battle 73-36. Douglas had too much balance for Johnson Williams last night. Noah Laws led the Bulldogs scoring with 25. Kenneth Pye added 18 and George Curry 17.

Winchester Evening Star
December 10, 1960

Take away the coach from a good basketball team and expect trouble. In Memorial Hospital for a spinal examination, Coach Bardsdale was as unhappy as might be expected over missing the trip. Although Mike Ford did a bang up job with the Bulldogs, they just didn't have it in losing to Simms 47-45. Top scoring honors went to Kenneth Pye 15 and Geroge Curry 12.

Winchester Evening Star
December 17, 1960

Douglas had a little trouble stopping Johnson WIlliams of Berryville last night on the Bulldogs home court as the score wnet to 63-36. Noah Laws was the Bulldogs high scorer with 26 points, Kenneth Pye added 11 and George Curry added 10. The Douglas JVs are still unbeaten after three games on the strenght of last night's 36-18 win.

Winchester Evening Star
January 7, 1961

A surprisingly strong Leesburg Douglass quint, knocked off Winchester's Douglas 70-56 last night on the winner's court. George Curry finished the night with 22 — his best performance of the year and came against the best team the Bulldogs have met so far. Noah Laws contributed 13.

Winchester Evening Star
January 12, 1961

Over anxious and inaccurate, the Bulldogs of Douglas fell before hard driving Lucy Simms 43-37 last night. As a result, the starting five may well be the substitutes the next few games as it was such youngsters as Charles "Pete" Washington who came through and this boy is straight from the junior varsity. Pete and Noah Laws both had 12 points.

Winchester Evening Star
January 14, 1961

Page Jackson of Charles Town happened along last night about the time Coach Ed Barksdale of Douglas had laid down the law to his Bulldogs because of a three game slump. The Bulldogs powered their way to an 87-35 victory. Noah Laws had 30, John Laws 17 and Pete Washington 15 for the Bulldogs. In the Junior game, Douglas came out on top 21-19. Clarence Curry led the way for the juniors with 9 points.

Winchester Evening Star
January 18, 1961

Douglas swings into State Quarter Finals by winning the district tournament. George Curry was named the most valuable player in the tournament because of his all around play. Douglas moves to Hampton, Virginia next Wednesday.

Winchester Evening Star
March 6, 1961

Two of the closest Midget League basketball races ever seen here will be decided tomorrow night at Douglas. The consolation game for third place will be decided between the Hawks and the Eagles. Their records are both 4-5. The title game will be between the Hoboes and the Royals both with records of 5-4. According to Coach Ed Barksdale, this is one basketball feature which the parents ought not to miss. The first game is set for 7:30 p.m.

Winchester Evening Star
March 20, 1961

The Douglas School Little League Basketball program will end its season tonight at 7:30 p.m. at the Douglas School. A picnic style supper will be served and trophies will be presented to teams holding first and second place in the league.

Winchester Evening Star
March 29, 1961

With a well balanced attack, Douglas was able to play it close to the vest last night in winning 50-45 at Page Jackson of Charles Town. The balance on the big team came from four shooters and a playmaker. Clarence Curry had 12 points, Robert Newman added 11, and John Laws and Lewis Long added 10 each. The Junior Varsity won their game 39-14. Norman Blowe chipped in 14 points and Franklin Washington added 12 for the JVs.

Winchester Evening Star
January 19, 1962
Douglas opened up all the stops at

Criser High of Front Royal last night for a twin bill victory the varsity winning 88-63 after the JVs had taken a 38-24 win for six in a row. Douglas ruled the backboards last night too, with Robert Newman, Louis Long, Noah and John Laws clearing everything. Paul Walker put on a Bob Cousey show for the fans as he fed Noah Laws for many of his 34 goals.

Winchester Evening Star
January 27, 1962

Douglas opened up a 41-25 half time margin against Lucy Simms of Harrisonburg last night and then floundered to a 65-32 league win here. The Bulldog JVs had matters better in hand with a 46-18 win over Simms for number six along an unbeaten trail.

Winchester Evening Star
January 31, 1962

Douglas had its chance for a revenge win against Rosenwald of Waynesboro last night, but the Bulldogs watched a victory sail out the window when Noah Laws' lay up spun the rim, dipped into the basket and then rolled back to the edge and down to the floor. Douglas was left holding the bag to the tune of 61-60. Leading scorers were Paul Walker 18, John Laws 13, and Clarence Curry and Noah Laws with 10 each.

Winchester Evening Star
February 14, 1962

Host Lucy Simms High of Harrisonburg was the seventh straight league victim of unbeaten Douglas of Winchester in a 73-46 victory last night to wind up the Bulldogs schedule. Overall the Bulldogs rolled to a 10-4 season but they couldn't be defeated in District 3 action. The three men in double figures were John Laws 20 points, Noah Laws 18, and Clarence Curry 16.

Winchester Evening Star
February 21, 1962
Douglas High proved the master of District 3 on Saturday at Criser of Front

Royal with two wins and a ticket to the State Group III quarter finals at Hampton. Early in the afternoon, the Bulldogs stoned Lucy Simms out of action 68-29 and advanced to the finals against Johnson Williams of Berryville. The Douglas Bulldogs won the championship game 68-32. The weekend tourney was the seventh victory in eight years for Douglas which lost only once on the ineligibility ruling. This year the Bulldogs had a 9-0 record in league play and 14-4 overall.

Winchester Evening Star
March 5, 1962

Douglas walked into the heart of the floodland of Virginia yesterday and came out of its first 1962 tournament game with an impressive 54-49 win over Rosenwald of Waynesboro, the school which had trimmed the Bulldogs twice during regular season action. Noah Laws had 24 points, 17 rebounds and 8 blocked shots, Paul Walker had 19 and Louis Long added 13.

Winchester Evening Star
March 9, 1962

After running into some rough snags yesterday, Douglas High of Winchester tore Hamilton High of King William apart by a margin of 82-59 and moved into the state championship round against Booker T. Washington of Staunton. It appeared that Douglas would have a bye into the finals when Hamilton didn't show up for its first game. The Bulldogs had just finished lunch and were told they had five minutes to dress and be on the floor. That took some hustling and there was no time for warm ups. Noah Laws had 20 points, John Laws had 16, and Clarence Curry had 14.

Winchester Evening Star
March 10, 1962

Douglas drops overtime duel against Booker T. Washington of Staunton, Virginia for state Group III Championship. Noah Laws was named outstanding tournament player. Going for the rebounds with Noah were Louis Long and Clarence Curry, while Paul Walker quarterbacked such a fine game that he was picked to the starting five along with Noah. In fact Noah and Paul (as did their teammates) that the huge crowd of 3,000 gave the Bulldogs a standing ovation at the end of the game.

Winchester Evening Star
March 12, 1962

Douglas wins 3rd Game, Defeats Johnson Williams 28-6. This is their third win of the season. Three touchdowns came from tosses from Clarence Curry to Noah Laws and the fourth from Curry himself. Coach Barksdale cited offensive linemen Bob Long, Herman Grimes, Russell Roberts, Ron Nelson, Andy Roberts and Wayne King for their outstanding play. In addition Barksdale credited Johnny Alsberry, Richard Woodson, Charles Finley and Joe Willis for their good showing on defense.

Winchester Evening Star
Ocober 8, 1962

The Douglas High School win streak was snapped yesterday by Cardoza High of Washington, D.C. 18-12 at Washington, D.C.

Winchester Evening Star
October 27, 1962

Douglas High with Homecoming scheduled for tomorrow may have to face Carver of Culpepper without the services of quarterback, Clarence Curry. If he cannot make it, Coach Barksdale will shift flanker back, Noah Laws, to the quarterback slot. Fullback, Joe Jackson, will again carry the brunt of the Bulldogs running attack.

Winchester Evening Star
November 4, 1962

Douglas suffers a 14-7 Homecoming loss to Carver of Culpepper. Louis Long registered the 6 points when he took a pass from Noah Laws and Joe Jackson rammed over with the extra point. This defeat, Douglas last game of the season, was the Bulldogs second against five wins. Simone Toliver was crowned Douglas Homecoming queen by senior footballer, Louis Long.

Winchester Evening Star
November 10, 1962

Douglas Seen Improving Last Year's 14-5 Record. Barksdale has a tall squad, headed by 6'4" Noah Laws. The remaining starting five will all stand over 6' and could be Clarence Curry (6'1"), Louis Long (6'), Paul Williams (6'4") and Charles Jackson (6'2"). His reserves are led by Norman Blowe (5'11"), Herman Grimes (6'3"), Leroy Woodson (5'8"), Robert Long (5'10"), Richard Woodson (5'9") and Randolph Martin (the shrimp of the crew at 5'-6"). Douglas only has 14 games on its regular slate this go-round.

Winchester Evening Star
November 29, 1962

Douglas wins opener 50-44 at the foul line over Lucy Simms of Harrisonburg at their gym. Noah Laws and Charles Jackson shared top scoring honors with 14 each. Louis Long contributed 12.

Winchester Evening Star
December 8, 1962

Douglas makes it two in a row with win over Criser of Front Royal. Top scorers were Noah Laws with 27, Clarence Curry with 19 and Paul Williams with 17.

Winchester Evening Star
December 15, 1962

Douglas won its third game of the season without a loss last night by overwhelming a hapless Page Jackson of Charles Town team 86-26 here. It was a case of too much height, a superb defense and a shooting eye that wasn't half bad for Coach Ed Barksdales' cagers. Tops scorer went to Clarence "Butch" Curry with 21, Noah Laws with 20, Charles Jackson with 12, and Paul Williams with 10. The Bulldogs pulled down 43 rebounds. Louis Long led with 12, Noah Laws and Paul Williams had 10 each.

Winchester Evening Star
January 3, 1963

Douglas scores at will in 73-20 romp over Lucy Simms. Noah Laws led all scorers with 22, Clarence Curry added 20 and Charles Jackson added 15. This win gave the Bulldogs a 5-0 record and left them as odds on favorites to romp all the way to the district championship.

Winchester Evening Star
January 12, 1963

Douglas sets field goal record in 122-14 victory over West Luray. Noah Laws led the way with 23, Clarence Curry 22, Paul Williams 14, Herman "Pete" Grimes 13, and Louis Long and Norman Blowe with 12 each. The Douglas girls won its only game in a preliminary 31-14.

Winchester Evening Star
January 18, 1963

Douglas High school came from behind the first quarter at Berryville last night to beat Johnson Williams 51-36. Noah Laws scored 20, Clarence Curry 14, and Paul Williams added 11. Douglas JV lost their contest 25-22.

Winchester Evening Star
January 19, 1963

Undefeated Douglas Bulldogs put their 7-0 record on the line at home against Carver of Culpeper.

Winchester Evening Star
January 22, 1963

Douglas Bulldogs last night accomplished a feat probably not too many fans outside their immediate rooting section expected: they defeated defending State Group III champions Booker T. Washington of Staunton - 53-43. The Bulldogs won with ease without Noah Laws because of foul trouble. The steady play of Charles Jackson, Norman Blowe, Paul Williams and the alert floor game of Clarence Curry was enough to offset Noah Laws. Top scorers were Paul Williams 16, Charles Jackson 12 and Norman Blowe 10.

Winchester Evening Star
February 19, 1963

Douglas High of Winchester had its 12 game win streak broken in Staunton last night 52-51. Coach Barksdale called this the most disgraceful game ever played and that he would not renew athletic relations with winning Booker T. Washington.

Winchester Evening Star
February 21, 1963

Douglas warmed up for its debut Saturday morning in the District 3 tournament by beating Criser of Front Royal 72-25 here last night. Coach Ed Barksdale cleared his bench using all 10 players and eight of them scored. Noah Laws led the winners with 19, Paul Williams followed with 16, and Clarence Curry added 14. The district tournament will be held Friday night and Saturday at the armory.

Winchester Evening Star
February 27, 1963

Douglas High School won its second Virginia Group II, District 1 basketball crown here Saturday night by defeating Johnson Williams of Berryville 80-57. At the end of the third period the score was tied 39-39. In the final period, the Bulldogs caught fire and ran through a streak that saw them register 33 points in the final period. Noah Laws led Douglas in scoring with 27, Clarence Curry 16, Louis Long 15 and Paul Williams finished with 12. Noah Laws won the Elks Club trophy for the "outstanding player" in the tournament.

Winchester Evening Star
March 4, 1963

Douglas High School is not going to have much of a football team this season. Not a poor record, it's just that there won't be many boys out for the team, according to head Coach Ed Barksdale. Added to this is the fact that the Bulldogs have so far definitely scheduled only two games with three other possibilities. Coach Barksdale in his 12th season at Douglas has compiled a 65-13-5 record in his 11 campaigns here.

Winchester Evening Star
September 20, 1963

Douglas, bulwarked by a stand out defense, struck for a second period touchdown and held on to upset the experts and Hoffman Boston here on Saturday by 6-0. Clarence Curry connected with Norman Blowe on a 15 yard pass for the only score in the game.

Winchester Evening Star
September 23, 1963

Douglas was over powered by a bigger and tougher Burley High School eleven last night and Douglas came out on the short end of a 33-6 game. Noah Laws scored the only touchdown for Douglas.

Winchester Evening Star
September 28, 1963

Clarence Curry sparked Douglas of Winchester to a 45-14 romp over Douglass of Leesburg at Leesburg on Friday night by scoring four touchdowns – one after returning from a hurried visit to the hospital following a second quarter injury. Noah Laws ran for two touchdowns and passed to Norman Blowe for a third touchdown.

Winchester Evening Star
October 26, 1963

Douglas Bulldogs homecoming loss to Cardoza 12-7 closes the abbreviated season. Douglas scored on a 16 yard pass from Noah Laws to George Dixon. Larry Banks scored the extra point. Douglas held Cardoza 7-0 until the end of the third quarter. Miss Lucille Roberts was crowned queen by Principal Kirk N. Gaskins. Lynn Carter was the crown bearer.

Winchester Evening Star
November 2, 1963

Douglas High Bulldogs, in their league opener against Lucy Simms of Harrisonburg, out scored their opponent 104-58 at Harrisonburg. Four of the Bulldog starters were in double figures for the evening; Noah Laws with 39, Clarence Curry 20, Norman Blowe 19, and Herman Grimes 15.

Winchester Evening Star
December 7, 1963

Douglas High turned loose a fierce scoring attack and Bulldog like defense against Johnson Williams of Berryville 93-35 at the Douglas gym. Noah Laws emerged as the game's top scorer with 35, Clarence Curry 21, William Beamer 12, and Herman Grimes 10.

Winchester Evening Star
December 12, 1963

Winchester Douglas High had a tougher time than expected at Leesburg but recorded its third straight victory 70-52. Noah Laws was top scorer for Douglas with 29, Herman Grimes added 15, Clarence Curry 12, and Norman Blowe 10.

Winchester Evening Star
December 18, 1963

Douglas Bulldogs coast to an easy win over Criser of Front Royal at Front Royal 79-42. Douglas netted 34 points in the opening eight minutes and held a 34-6 first quarter lead. The three men in double figures were Noah Laws 36, Norman Blowe 18, and William Beamer 10.

Winchester Evening Star
January 4, 1964

Douglas was handed their second defeat of the season by Luther Jackson 73-53. The Bulldogs journeyed to Fairfax without their leading scorer Noah Laws. Norman Blowe was the high man for Douglas with 15, Herman Grimes 11, and Clarence Curry 10.

Winchester Evening Star
January 30, 1964

Douglas romped pass Criser of Front Royal 84-50 and upped its perfect V.I.A. record to 5-0. Leading scorers for Douglas were Noah Laws 25, Clarence Curry 22, and Norman Blowe 20.

Winchester Evening Star
February 1, 1964

Douglas won the contest against Carver of Culpeper 95-65 last night. Noah Laws scored 32, Clarence Curry 23, Norman Blowe 16, and William Beamer 12.

Winchester Evening Star
February 21, 1964

Douglas of Winchester, playing without Noah Laws most of the game, upended Douglass of Leesburg 77-61. Clarence Curry scored 21, Herman Grimes 19, and Noah Laws and Norman Blowe 16 each.

Winchester Evening Star
February 26, 1964

The Douglas Bulldogs were victorious at Criser of Front Royal winning the district championship 10 in a row. The Bulldogs topped Johnson Williams 80-59 in the semi-final game and Criser 77-53 in the windup round. Ernest Turner of Johnson Williams was named most valuable player and Noah Laws won the Daniel J. Farrar Elks Club trophy as the best performer of the match.

Winchester Evening Star
March 9, 1964

The Douglas Bulldogs were eliminated from the Group II basketball tournament at Hampton, Virginia by Booker T. High 76-43.

Winchester Evening Star
March 13, 1964

The high scoring duo of William Beamer (27) and Norman Blowe (23) combined for 50 points last night to topple Douglas of Leesburg 77-58. This win placed the locals 2-1 on the season. Douglas bagged 31 big fielders while holding the Loudoun County outfit to just 19 goals.

Winchester Evening Star
January 13, 1965

Douglas evened their record last night by downing West Luray 81-47. The Bulldogs are now three and three on the season. The Bulldogs took 86 shots from the floor but only connected on 35 of them. At the charity strip, Douglas hit 11 of 13. Norman Blowe led the Douglas team with 31, Irvin Baltimore added 14, and William Beamer added 16.

Winchester Evening Star
January 30, 1965

Carver High nipped Douglas 106-104 in the area's wildest scoring game of this year. Douglas had four men in double figures: Norman Blowe-38, William Beamer-27, Irvin Baltimore 17, and Larry Banks 15. The rebounding of Blowe, Harry Williams and Banks was another highlight for Coach Barksdale's boys.

Winchester Evening Star
February 3, 1965

Douglas waltzed over West Luray High on Luray's court last night 69-42. The high scoring duo of Norman Blowe (28) and William Beamer (19) pulled down the laurels for the Kent Streeters. The rebounding of Joe Cook and Larry Banks was outstanding. The floor game of Irvin Baltimore and Randolph Martins was sharp also. Paul Washington had 21 for the Douglas JVs in their 54-41 win.

Winchester Evening Star
February 5, 1965

Carver did it again, by the same margin too, as Douglas lost to the Culpeper quint 71-69 last night. William Beamer went on a great 46 point scoring binge for the Bulldogs in a fabulous display of shooting of ball hawking. Norman Blowe contributed 15 points for Douglas.

Winchester Evening Star
February 10, 1965

Douglas edged arch-rival Johnson-Williams 65-63 in a frenzied affair at Douglas Saturday night. William Beamer paced the Douglas attack with 28 points, Norman Blowe had 18, and Harry Willliams 13.

Winchester Evening Star
February 15, 1965

Johnson-Williams pinned the first defeat on Douglas since 1959 in their annual rivalry Saturday night by tripping the Bulldogs 68-67. This victory tied the Tigers and Bulldogs in league play with a 5-3 mark.

Top scorers for the Bulldogs were: Norman Blowe 23, William Beamer 18, and Harry Williams 13.

Winchester Evening Star
March 2, 1965

Norman Blowe was named to the First Team and William Beamer to the Second Team in the "65 Evening Star All Area Team.

Winchester Evening Star
March 3, 1965

Douglas captured the Virginia Interscholastic Association-District 1 Championship on Saturday by clipping arch rival Johnson-Williams and Lucy Simms. In the Douglas-Johnson-Williams game 61-49, high scorers for Douglas were; Norman Blowe-16, Harry Williams-14 and Robert Baltimore-13. In the Douglas – Lucy Simms game 53-47, high scorers for Douglas were William Beamer and Norman Blowe with 14 each.

Winchester Evening Star
March 8, 1965

Douglas High ended their season on a sour note yesterday by taking a 71-42 thumping from Booker T. Washington High of Staunton in the first round of the Virginia Interscholastic Association Tourney at Hampton Institute. William Beamer with 16 and Norman Blowe with 12 points led the double digit parade for the locals.

Winchester Evening Star
March 11, 1965

Douglas fields 7 men to play 6 game schedule. From Coach Barksdale, "We only decided two weeks ago to play basketball this season. This is our experimental year. We will feature a go-go offense. We have speed and good ball handlers. The boys know the game and play intelligent basketball. We have some good shooters."

Winchester Evening Star
November 30, 1965

With Bill Beamer 5 feet 9, the tallest Bulldog, Douglas Coach Edwin Barksdale turned loose his scurrying mites against a taller, slower Douglass Team from Leesburg. The Bulldogs won 60-40. Beamer led the home team with 21 points, Randolph Martin, Robert Baltimore and Bob Stern each contributed 12 points to the Douglas total.

Winchester Evening Star
December 4, 1965

Ernest Turner outdueled Douglas' Robert Baltimore in their arch rival hardwood contest last night as Johnson-Williams whipped Douglas 78-72. Douglas was led by Robert Baltimore-31, Robert Stern-12, William Beamer 11 and Randolph Martin 10

Winchester Evening Star
December 11, 1965

Douglas School May Day event in 1953. The member of the team from left to right: Floyd Burks (standing alone), Louis Allen Washington with James Carter (holding), Floyd Walker with John Carter Finley (holding), Robert Burks with Beverly Gaskins (holding), David Clinton with unidentified (holding), and Walter Peyton (standing alone.) 555-198 thl

The girls and JV (Junior Varsity) Teams played their games before the Varsity Boys team and were also coached by Coach Barksdale.The girls' team averaged 3 games per year and was 14-7.

Information on the JV games was not always reported to the Winchester Evening Star but they also had winning seasons.

Coach Barksdale also ran a Saturday morning Midget League for young boys and they were often coached by older boys.

Edwin K. Barksdale

(February 25, 1927 - March 21, 1974)

Teacher and athletic coach at Douglas School c. 1950. (555-155)

THE DOUGLAS FOOTBALL RECORDS
THE BARKSDALE YEARS
1953–1966

YEAR	WON	LOST	TIED	SCORED	ALLOWED
1953	5	0		144	6
1954	7	1		207	12
1955	4	3		74	52
1956	2	4		51	73
1957	2	4	1	60	50
1958	2	1	2	86	18
1959	4	0		136	7
1960	7	1		326	55
1961	7	1		393	26
1962	6	2		87	68
1963	2	2		64	59
1964	No Team				
1965	No Team				
Totals	48	19	3	1628	426

TRI-STATE CHAMPIONS
    1953-1954

DISTRICT CHAMPIONS
1959 -1960- 1961-1962

UNDEFEATED TEAMS
    1953 and 1959

DOUGLAS BASKETBALL RECORDS
THE BARKSDALE YEARS
1953–1966

YEAR	WON	LOST	POINTS SCORED	POINTS ALLOWED
1953-4	Not Available			
1954-5	14	8	1342	1015
1955-6	9	8	709	626
1956-7	14	7	1205	989
1957-8	14	3	1046	774
1958-9	14	3	1032	888
1959-60	9	1	593	436
1960-61	8	6	787	585
1961-2	11	5	1069	771
1962-3	13	2	1117	586
1963-4	11	4	1130	842
1964-5	8	7	1020	896
1965-6	3	7	515	573
Totals	128	61	11,565	8981

DISTRICT CHAMPIONS – 10
1955-1959 & 1961-1965
Lost in 1960
(Due to ineligibity ruling)

REGION WINNERS - 4
1957 - 1958 - 1959 - 1962

STATE RUNNER-UPS – 2
1958 & 1962 (Lost in double overtime to Booker T. Washington of Staunton 46-45.)

1st Undefeated Season – 1953 Douglas Football, 5 -0

Michael Ford and Hubert Stephenson co-captains

Points		Douglas Points	Other
Sept. Luray		47	0
Oct. 12	Culpeper	6	0
Oct. 15	Culpeper	45	0
Oct. 26	Page – Jackson	19	6
Nov. 6	Page-Jackson	<u>27</u>	<u>0</u>
Total		144	6

2nd Undefeated Season – 1959 Douglas Football, 4 -0

Points		Douglas Points	Other
Sept. 25	Lucy Simms – Harrisonburg, VA	54	7
Oct. 24	Lucy Simms – Harrisonburg, VA	34	0
Oct. 30	Douglass – Leesburg, VA	21	0
Nov. 6	Jeanne Dean – Manassas, VA	<u>27</u>	<u>0</u>
		136	7

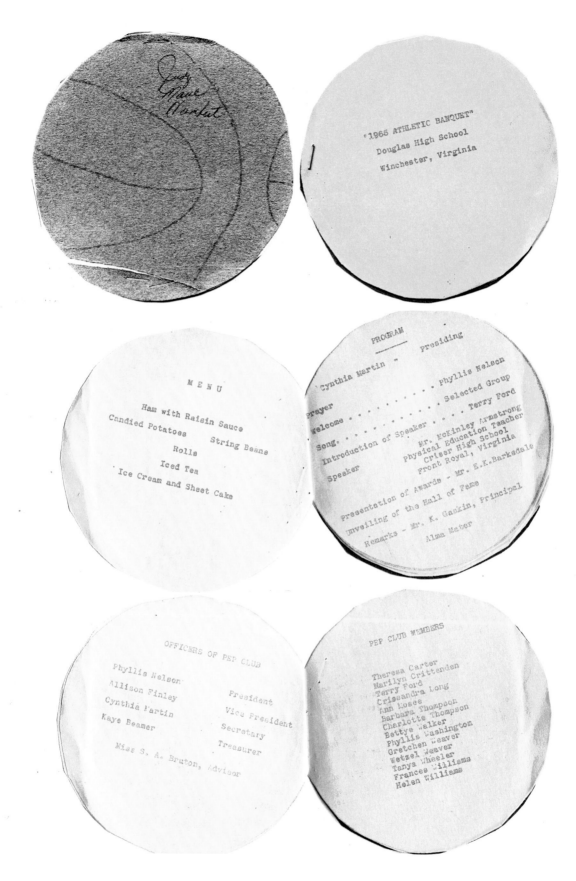

"1965 ATHLETIC BANQUET"
Douglas High School
Winchester, Virginia

M E N U

Ham with Raisin Sauce
Candied Potatoes   String Beans
Rolls
Iced Tea
Ice Cream and Sheet Cake

PROGRAM

Cynthia Martin -   Presiding

Prayer . . . . Phyllis Nelson
Welcome . . . . Selected Group
Song . . . . Terry Ford
Introduction of Speaker . . . . Mr. McKinley Armstrong
                                 Physical Education Teacher
                                 Criser High School
Speaker   Front Royal, Virginia

Presentation of Awards - Mr. E.K. Barksdale
Unveiling of the Hall of Fame
Remarks - Mr. K. Gaskin, Principal
                    Alma Mater

OFFICERS OF PEP CLUB

Phyllis Nelson
Allison Finley   President
Cynthia Martin   Vice President
Kaye Beamer   Secretary
                          Treasurer

Miss S. A. Bruton, Advisor

PEP CLUB MEMBERS

Theresa Carter
Marilyn Crittenden
Terry Ford
Criseandra Long
Ann Losee
Barbara Thompson
Charlotte Thompson
Bettye Walker
Phyllis Washington
Gretchen Weaver
Wetzel Weaver
Tanya Wheeler
Frances Williams
Helen Williams

1965 Athletic Banquet
program (555-178)

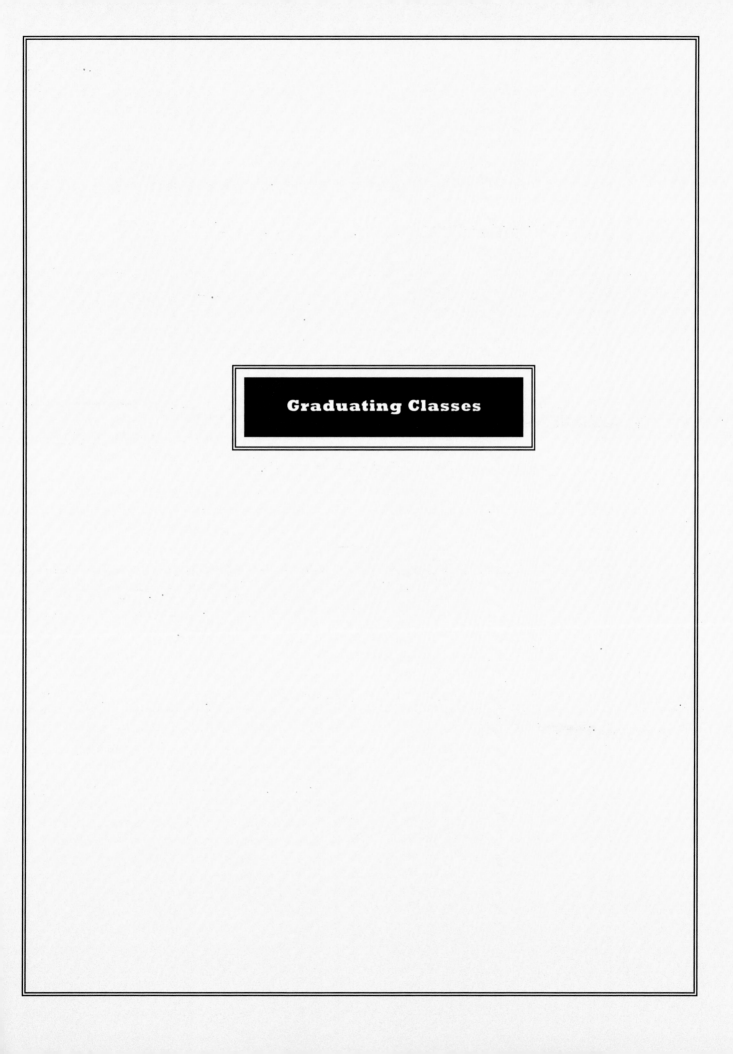

Graduating Classes

Graduation

City Public Schools,
Winchester, Virginia.

Grammar Department.

FINAL EXAMINATION, JUNE, 190

NAME Hester Davis

GRADE 5th

Spelling	
Reading	
Writing	
Dictation and Plain Copy	85
Composition	70
Arithmetic	
Geography (Manual)	
Geography of Virginia	75
Grammar	
History of United States	
Stories from Virginia History	
Physiology	
General Spelling	
General Character of Work	
Average Standing	
Rank in Class	
Attendance	
Deportment	

EXPLANATION OF GRADES: From 95 to 100 excellent; 90 to 95 good; 80 to 90 fair; 70 to 80 low; below 70 unsatisfactory.
REQUIREMENTS FOR PROMOTION: Pupils must receive at least 70 per ct. on each study and an average standing of 75 per ct. for promotion.

REMARKS:

Days absent during the term 10

M H Quiett Teacher.

1900s Report card for Hester Davis (555-165)

School certificate for C. Louisa Tokes. "Public School of Winchester, Virginia - Annual Examination, June 1902. - This Certificate of Distinction - is awarded to: C. Louisa Tokes - For having completed the Grammar School Course during the / Session Ending June 1902.- J. C. Van Fossen, Principal." (737-7)

Class of 1907

NO PICTURES OR ARTICLES AVAILABLE

The session of 1905-1906 of the colored public school of Winchester, John H. Quiett, principal, came to a close this morning, diplomas being awarded to six graduates.

A feature of the closing was the address by Prof. N.W. Brakett, the principal of Storer College, at Harpers Ferry, W.Va., one of the foremost educational institutions of colored people in the South. Addresses were also delivered by Revs. Carter, Curry, and Hargrove of Winchester. All the speakers confined their remarks to the idea that in work lies the salvation of the colored race.

June 15, 1906

Newspaper article from *Winchester Evening Star* (555-N02)

PUBLIC SCHOOLS
O F
Winchester, - - - - Virginia.

ANNUAL EXAMINATION, JUNE 1905.

This Certificate of Distinction

IS AWARDED TO

Harry Jacklin

For having completed the Grammar School Course during the
Session ending June, 1905.

Jno. H. Quiett Principal.

Class of 1909-1911

NO PICTURES OR ARTICLES
AVAILABLE

Class of 1913-1917

NO PICTURES OR ARTICLES
AVAILABLE

THE COLORED SCHOOL FINALS

The colored public school of this city closed on Friday evening, after a most successful session under the management of Prof. John Quiett and his faithful assistants.

There were seven pupils graduated at the closing of this term, and they were Pauline Jackson, Francis Culett, Virginia Morgan, Funnie Washington, Wesley Turner and Harry Hamer.

The exercises were held in the Free Will Baptist Church, and were attended by all the patrons of the school. A number of white people also attended the exercises, which were much enjoyed.

The teachers of the school wish to express their thanks to both their white and colored friends who so cheerfully contributed towards the establishment of a library at the school.

Winchester Evening Star
June 17, 1912. p. 5

CLASS MOTTO--"EXCELSIOR"

CLASS ROLL

META EVANS

RACHEL JACKSON

ROBERT DAVIS

LAURENCE PHILLIPS

ELIZABETH JENNINGS

MADISON BRISCOE

KIRK GASKINS

TAYLOR FINLEY

RICHARD WASHINGTON

SARAH HARMON

CLASS COLORS--BLUE AND WHITE

PROGRAM

OVERTURE . . . . Orchestra
ANTHEM . . . . Choral Club
INVOCATION
ANTHEM . . . . Choral Club
SALUTATORY . . . . Madison Briscoe
ESSAY . . . . Laurence Phillips
ORATION . . . . Robert Davis
SOLO . . . . Elizabeth Jennings
ORATION . . . . Taylor Finley
VIOLIN INTERMEZZO . . . . Kirk Gaskins
CLASS PROPHECY . . . . Richard Washington
CLASS HISTORY . . . . Rachel Jackson
VALEDICTORY . . . . Meta Evans
SOLO—Au Revoir . . . . Sarah Harmon
ADDRESS
PRESENTATION OF CERTIFICATES . Supt. Leslie D. Cline
CHORUS
ORCHESTRA.

Commencement
program 1918
(555-166b).
Cover (555-166a)

Annual Commencement
of the
Douglas Graded School
Winchester, Va.
at
Mt. Carmel Baptist Church
Tuesday, June 11, 1918
at 8:30 p. m.
You are cordially invited to
attend these exercises
D. W. Gibson, Principal

Class of 1920-1921

NO PICTURES OR ARTICLES
AVAILABLE

Class Roll

KATHLEEN WATKINS BANKS
MARGARETTA NEOMIA CARTER
VIVIAN VIRGINIA CHAMP
NAOMI RUTH FISHER
POWELL WILLARD GIBSON, Jr.
VIRGINIA CABLE GREENE
CECIL MAINE PEARSON
RUTH VIRGINIA STEPHENSON
MARY ELOISE STEPHENSON
HESTER SARAH TOKUS
CORA VIOLET TOKUS

Programme

Chorus	School Choir
Invocation	
Salutatory	Kathleen W. Banks
Class History	Hester S. Tokus
Vocal Solo	Ruth V. Stephenson
Class Prophecy	Cora V. Tokus
Oration	Cecil M. Pearson
Class Poem	Virginia C. Greene
Chorus	School Choir
Essay	Mary E. Stephenson
Oration	Powell W. Gibson, Jr.
Vocal Solo	Margaretta N. Carter
Declamation	Naomi R. Fisher
Valedictory	Virginia V. Champ
Address	Dr. H. T. McDonald, Pres. Storer College, [Harpers Ferry

Douglas School Commencement Program, June 16, 1922

Winchester Public Schools
JOHN HANDLEY FOUNDATION

This Certificate is awarded to

Powell Willard Gibson jr.

in acknowledgment of the successful completion of the work of the *ninth* Grade
of the Winchester Public Schools.

_____
Superintendent

_____
President School Board

_____
Principal

_____
President Handley Trustees

Commencement
program 1922
(555-168)

Powell W. Gibson
Diploma (555-169)

Douglas 125

Class Roll

LOUISA LAURA CARTER

WILLIAM BRISCOE JENNINGS

HELEN MATILDA JENNINGS

GEORGE EMANATHRIS LAVENDER

CHARLES HENRY LEWIS

NEWTON THOMAS THOMPSON

JOSEPHINE MARY WHEELER

GEORGE EDWARD WASHINGTON

Program

Orchestra

Chorus . . . . School Choir

Invocation

Chorus . . . . School Choir

Salutatory . . . . George E. Washington

Class History . . . . Josephine M. Wheeler

Oration . . . . William B. Jennings

Vocal Solo . . . . Louisa L. Carter

Oration . . . . George E. Lavender

Chorus . . . . School Choir

Class Poem . . . . Helen M. Jennings

Orchestra

Oration . . . . Newton T. Thompson

Valedictory . . . . Charles H. Lewis

Address . . . . Dr. John M. Gandy
Pres. State Normal School, Petersburg, Va.

Douglas School Commencement Program, June 13, 1923

(555-170)

Class of 1924

NO PICTURES OR ARTICLES
AVAILABLE

Douglas School is Operated on High Standard

Public is Invited to Inspect the Industrial Exhibit During Tomorrow

The Douglas School of the Winchester Public School System is bringing to a close tomorrow evening its most successful year. The principal, P.W. Gibson, has put forth a great deal of effort to bring his school up to the highest possible standard under existing conditions.

A well prepared program will be rendered, beginning at 8 p.m., as follows:

Chorus, American hymn
Invocation
Chorus, American hymn
Salutatory, Mary F. Hogans
Class history, Leon W. Boles
Oration, Lawrence A. Myers
Chorus, *God Ever Glorious*
Class prophecy, Maria N. Conley
Oration, Julian E. Myers
Solo, Mary V. Finley
Class will, Grace H. Greene
Chorus, *The Exile*
Oration, Walter S. Carter
Solo, Elenora G. Finley
Class Poem, Ruth I. Washington
Piano solo, Katie B. Washington
Valedictory, Hugh N. Williams
Presentation of certificates, Superintendant. H.S. Duffey
Chorus, *Spirit of Peace*
Address, Garnett C. Wilkinson, Superintendent of Colored Schools, Washington D.C.
Chorus, *National Negro Anthem Benediction*
Orchestra

During Wednesday, from 9 a.m. to 6 p.m., the school will have on exhibition a great deal of interesting material, which is the product of their industrial department. Anyone going to the building at these hours will be able to see exhibits of woodwork, sewing, painting and drawing. The community at large is urgently requested to visit the school, in order that they may obtain some idea of the eminent work which is being done.

Twelve students will graduate this year. The class roll is as follows: Leon Warner Boles, Maria Naomi Conley, Walter Stanford Carter, Mary Virginia Finley, Elenora Gaskins Finley, Hazel Grace Greene, Mary Frances Hogans, Lawrence Albert Myers, Julian Edward Myers, Ruth Isabella Washington, Katie Belle Washington and Hugh Nelson Williams."

Winchester Evening Star
June 4, 1925, p. 3

Class of 1926

NO PICTURES OR ARTICLES
AVAILABLE

(555-171a)

Program

Orchestra

Chorus..Choir

Invocation

Chorus..Choir

Salutatory........................Sarah F. Fletcher

Class History.............Katherine D. Shelton

Oration................................James A. Waldon

Chorus..Choir

Class Phrophecy............Virginia E. Shelton

Solo.............................Elizabeth M. Nickens

Valedictory...................Clifford S. Brooks

Address

Chorus..Choir

Benediction

Class Roll

Clifford Shorts Brooks

Sarah Frances Fletcher

Elizabeth Meade Nickens

Katherine Dora Shelton

Virginia Elizabeth Shelton

James Albert Waldon

(555-171b)

Douglas School graduating class of 1927, nine grades. This was the last class graduating from the Old Stone Presbyterian Church at 306 East Piccadilly Street. According to the 1927 program, the students were Clifford S. Brooks, Sarah F. Fletcher, Elizabeth M. Nicken, Katherine D. Shelton, Virginia E. Shelton, and James A. Waldon. The only positive identification is Katherine D. Shelton (2nd from left.) (1706-24)

Douglas School graduating class of 1928. According to a June 12, 1928 news article, class members were: Evelyn Banks - salutatorian, Corneilus Conley, Beatrice Finley, Josephine R. Jackson - valedictorian, James W. Coles, Julian Jackson, Thomas Greene, and John Washington. Only positive identification: Beatrice Finley (middle front row), and John Washington (left on 2nd row.) (1493-167)

"Colored School Finals Attract a Record Crowd"

"Prof. Sampson Advocates Curriculum of Academic and Industrial Courses"

"The first commencement of the Douglas Junior High School to be held in the new building drew the largest crowd last night of the colored race yet assembled in Winchester for a similar event, and the program presented justified such an attendance, for it was the best the school has ever offered.

The address to the graduates was delivered by Prof. George M. Sampson, and he made an able exposition of the past development and future hopes for Negro education, soundly advocating improved schooling facilities in the matter of better buildings, better trained teachers and compulsory attendance, together with a curriculum offering academic and industrial courses.

Subject Ably Presented – Professor Sampson made a decidedly able presentation of the subject and proved to the audience by his subject matter, phraseology and delivery that he is one of the outstanding educators among his race.

Each member of the graduating class had a part in the program and contributed his or her part toward the success of the evening.

The salutatorian was Evelyn Banks, the class prophet Cornelius S. Conley, the class poet Beatrice Finley, the class historian Josephine R. Jackson, the valedictorian James W. Coles, and the orators Julian W. Jackson and Thomas L. Greene. John L. Washington made his contribution by a well-rendered saxophone solo.

The musical program added much to the evening's entertainment, numbers being furnished by a mixed chorus under the direction of Mrs. Anna Quiett Brooks and by the orchestra, an organization which has made wonderful progress and deserves the encouragement of the people of this community.

Certificates Presented – The certificates of graduation were presented by Supt. H.S. Duffey with appropriate remarks.

The program was presided over by Prof. Powell W. Gibson, and he and his teaching associates and pupils were to be sincerely congratulated upon the success of the occasion.

This year's graduates of the Douglas Junior High School are Evelyn Love Banks, Cornelius Samuel Conley, James Willard Coles, Beatrice Lee Finley, Thomas Leonard Greene, Josephine Randolph Jackson, Julian Worcester Jackson and John Lewis Washington.

Handiwork Display Excites Interest – In addition to presenting a commencement program of unusual merit, pupils of the school also had on display a large collection of their handiwork, which excited a great deal of interest and high praise.

Especially noteworthy were the displays in the departments of domestic science and manual training. The various articles were labeled with the names of the pupils who had executed the work and after the exercises the articles were distributed among the students for their keeping."

Winchester Evening Star
June 12, 1928

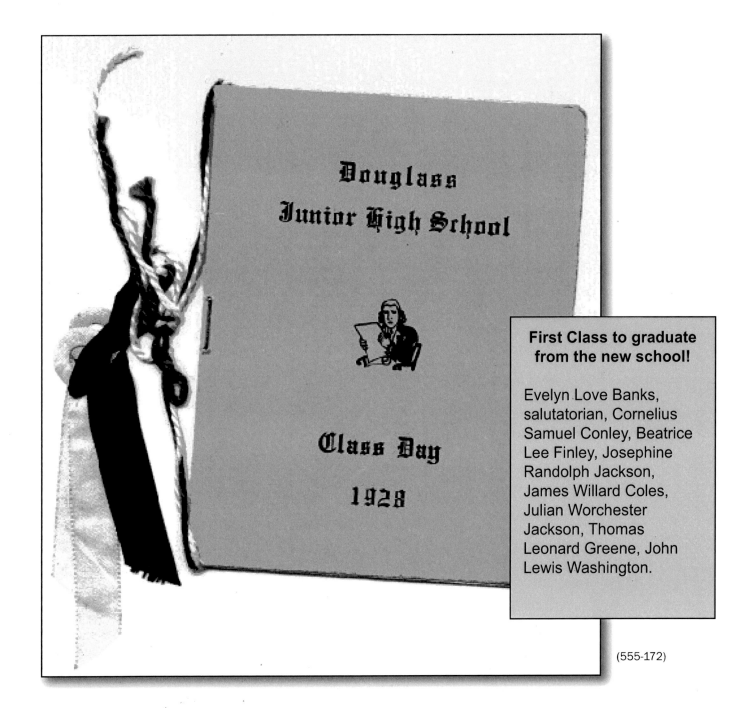

Douglass
Junior High School

Class Day

1928

First Class to graduate from the new school!

Evelyn Love Banks, salutatorian, Cornelius Samuel Conley, Beatrice Lee Finley, Josephine Randolph Jackson, James Willard Coles, Julian Worchester Jackson, Thomas Leonard Greene, John Lewis Washington.

(555-172)

Class of 1929

NO PICTURES OR ARTICLES
AVAILABLE

1930

Class Roll

Florence Rebecca Shelton
Gertrude Anita Brooks
Katherine Marie Greene
Louise Virginia Swift
Mary Louise Wilhoit
Randolph Warenton Robinson
Ruth Cornelia Burks
Sadie Amelia Finley
Sylvia Tralice Dixon

Program

Chorus
Invocation
Chorus
Salutatory - - Mary L. Wilhoit
Vocal Solo - - Ruth C. Burks
Class Poem - - Louise V. Swift
Inst. Solo - Gertrude A. Brooks
Class History - - Florence Shelton
Vocal Solo - - Sadie A. Finley
Class Phophecy - Sylvia T. Dixon
Class Will - Katherine M. Greene
Class Song
Valedictory - Randolph W. Robinson
Presentation of Certificates
Supt. H. S. Duffey
Address - - Prof. J. Francis Gregory
Miner Normal School Wash. D. C.
Chorus - - - - Choir
Benediction

(555-173)

"Douglas School Commencement to Begin Tonight"

"Five pupils will be graduated from Douglas School, colored, commencement exercises beginning this evening and terminating with the awarding of certificates Wednesday at 8:30 p.m.

At 8:30 p.m. tonight, a program will be rendered by the pupils of Douglas School as follows: chorus, by the school; dance of the fairies, primary grades; radio play, fourth and fifth grades; play, *The Patron of Art*, advanced girls, and an exhibit of industries.

Wednesday evening, at 8:30 o'clock, the final exercises are scheduled. The program will be: welcome, Lucille Hogans; spring songs, primary boys; dance of the sunbeams; *How to Dress Well*, Mary E. Ford; chorus, *O Sole Mio*; *The Importance of Studying Foods*, Frances L. Finley; address; presentation of certificates, Superintendant. Garland R. Quarles, Handley Schools; chorus, *Lift Every Voice and Sing*. Those who will receive certificates are Frances Lee Finley, Lucille Elizabeth Hogans, Eldridge Fairfax Wanzer, Harold Lawrence Williams and Joseph Herbert Willis."

Winchester Evening Star
June 8, 1931

Class of 1932-1933

NO PICTURES OR ARTICLES
AVAILABLE

Douglas School graduates (nine grades) class of 1934. Front row, left to right: Annie E. Turner, Frances K. Greene , Magnolia A. Williams (salutatorian), Elizabeth V. Cooke, Powell Willard Gibson (principal); second row, left to right: Jefferson W. Lewis, John W. Tokes, Lamont W. Carter, Gouverneur C. Pinn, Taylor Floyd Finley (teacher); thirrd row, left to right: Henry Moss Brooks, Rodman Turner (valedictorian), Amuel W. Jackson. (555-45)

"Exercises to be Held at Douglas School Tomorrow"

"Industrial Exhibit Open to the Public All Day – 11 to Graduate"

"Commencement exercises will be held at Douglas Junior High School at 8:30 Friday evening, when Superintendent Garland R. Quarles will present certificates to eleven graduates and a class day program will be held.

An unusually fine exhibit of industrial work completed by the students will be on display throughout the day Friday, according to P.W. Gibson, principal, and the grounds and buildings on North Kent street will be open to the public for inspection throughout Friday. The public is cordially invited to attend not only the commencement exercises but to visit the exhibit and inspect the grounds and building.

Evening Program – The evening program will be opened with a chorus. The invocation will follow and in the following order, the program consists of salutatory, Magnolia A. Williams; chorus, *Somebody's Knocking at Your Door*; oration, Gouveneaur C. Pinn; violin solo, Amuel W. Jackson; class poem, Frances K. Greene; class history, Elizabeth V. Cooke; vocal solo, Lamont W. Carter; class prophecy, Annie E. Turner; class will, Jefferson W. Lewis; class song, *Farewell to Thee*; oration, John W. Tokes; cornet solo, Henry M. Brooks, valedictory, Rodman L. Turner.

The presentation of certificates will follow and the program will be closed with the chorus, *Even Me*, and the benediction."

Winchester Evening Star
June 14, 1934

Class of 1935
Commencement
Program (555-174)

Douglas School graduates (nine grades) class of 1936. Front row, left to right: Josephine Shields, Madeline Burns, Ella V. Myers, Rachel Willis, Lillie Turner, Mildred Wanzer; second row, left to right: Charles Turner, Samuel Ford, Taylor F. Finley (teacher), Lovelena Lomax Marcus (teacher), Professor Powell W. Gibson (principal), Clarke Dixon, Mathew Davis, Samuel Walker. (1493-37)

"Douglas School to Close Friday"

"Rev. W.N. Holt is to Address Graduates at
Their Exercises"

"Commencement exercises of the Douglas Junior High School will be held at 7:30 o'clock Friday evening of this week at the new colored school building of North Kent street under the direction of the principal, Prof. Powell W. Gibson, assisted by his loyal corps of teachers. The exercises are open to the general public, and everyone is invited.

In addition to the commencement program, the school has on exhibition tomorrow and Friday a large and varied assortment of articles made by pupils in the departments of manual training and home economics. It is a very attractive display, showing what the boys and girls of that school can do in a practical way. Anyone interested in the development of the young colored is invited to see this exhibit.

Graduating Exercises – The graduating program Friday evening opens with a chorus by a large choir, followed by an invocation, another choral selection, and then the salutatory by James P. Washington. Following a song by the choir, the valedictory will be given by Bettie J. Anderson.

Certificates of graduation will be presented by Garland R. Quarles, superintendent of city schools, to the class of 1937. They are Bettie Josephine Anderson, Theda Louise Bundy, Mary Elizabeth Carter, Ida Mae Finley, Malissa Elizabeth Harris, Emily Page Johnson, Elizabeth G. Hester McGruder, Gladys Viana Martin, Robert Powell Johnson and James Pollard Washington.

The address to the class will be delivered by the Rev. W.N. Holt, pastor of John Mann Methodist Church, this city.

The exercises will close with a chorus by the choir and the benediction.

The class motto is "Lift As You Climb," and the class colors are blue and white, while the carnation was selected as the class flower.

Officers of the class of 1937 are: Emiley P. Johnson, president; Ellen J. Finley, vice-president; Bettie J. Anderson, secretary, and Elizabeth H. McGruder, treasurer."

Winchester Evening Star
June 9, 1937

Class of 1937

Certificates of graduation were received by Bettie Josephine Anderson, Theda Louise Bundy, Mary Elizabeth Carter, Ida Mae Finley, Malissa Elizabeth Harris, Emily Page Johnson, Elizabeth G. Hester McGruder, Gladys Viana Martin, Robert Powell Johnson and James Pollard Washington.

Douglas School graduating class of 1938, nine grades. Front row, left to right: Sarah Anderson, Lovelena Lomax Marcus (teacher), Amanda Herbert, Helen Burks, Virginia Cary, Mary Russell; second row, left to right: Taylor Floyd Finley (teacher), Louis Long, Frederick Taper, Houston Taylor, Marcellus Nickens, Thomas Turner, Morris Ford, Powell Willard Gibson (principa.) (555-46)

Class of 1939-1940

NO PICTURES OR ARTICLES
AVAILABLE

TENTH GRADE WAS ADDED

Douglas High School graduating class of 1941 and faculty. Front row, left to right: Hattie M. Lea (teacher), Velma Lewis (salutatorian), Alice Weaver, Portia Triplett, (valedictorian); second row, left to right: faculty: Mrs. Nerissa Wright, Francis M. Jackson, Thomas Haywood, Powell Willard Gibson, Kirk Nathaniel Gaskins Sr. (principal). Commencement address was given by Dr. Henry T. McDonald (not in photo), President, Storer College. Harpers Ferry, West Virginia. (555-47)

Douglas High School graduating class of 1942 and faculty. Front row, seated, left to right: Wardell Cartwright, Hattie Green, Mary Green, Earl Pinkett; second row, standing, faculty: left to right: Sterling Walker, Anna Quiett Brooks Tokes, Blanche Gibson Moten, Hattie M. Lea, Thomas Haywood, Lovelena Lomax Marcus, Francis M. Jackson, Nerissa Wright, Kirk N. Gaskins, Sr (principal). (555-48)

Douglas High School graduating class of 1943 and falculty. Front row, seated, left to right: Mary Louise Williams, Roland Harper, Weaver Banks, John Poulson (salutatorian), Vivienne Jackson (valedictorian); second row, standing, faculty, left to right: Francis M. Jackson , Hattie M. Lea , Blanche Gibson Moten, Lovelena Lomax Marcus, Thomas Haywood, Nerissa Wright, Anna Q. Brooks Tokes, Effie McKinney, Kirk N. Gaskins, Sr (principal). (555-49)

Douglas High School graduating class of 1944. Left to right: Lorraine Turner (salutatorian), Taylor Floyd Finley, Jr, Zelma Pinkett (valedictorian). (555-50)

Douglas High School graduating class of 1945. Front row, seated, left to right: Anna Wanzer (valedictorian), Ellen Williams, Louis Gaither, Lanier Turner (salutatorian), Alberta Washington, Madeléne Mitchell, second row, standing, left to right: Vivian Taper, Mary Wanzer, Alice Crawford (555-51)

Baccalaureate Service Sunday June 3, 3:00 pm; sermon by Rev. J. Dallas Jenkins (not in photo).of Luray, Virginia.

Graduation - Thursday, June 7, 8:00 pm.

Douglas High School graduating class of 1946. Left to right: Allene Williams, Sue Catlett (valedictorian), Josephine Catlett, Selma Williams (salutatorian), Elizabeth Nickens.

Rev. Alexander Easy (not in photo), Principal, Williams Training School, Berryville, delivered the Baccalaureate Sermon on June 2, 1946. Graduation was June 6, 1946, 9 pm. (555-52)

The Senior Class
of
Douglas High School
requests your presence
at the
Bacccalaureate Address
Sunday, June second
4.30 three o'clock P. M
and the
Commencement Exercises
Thursday evening, June sixth
nineteen hundred forty-six
eight-thirty o'clock
School Auditorium

CLASS MOTTO
"Not Finished, Just Begun"

CLASS ROLL
Jack Franklin Burks
Jane Iris Josephine Catlett
Sue Evelyn Catlett
Elizabeth Evalena Nickens
Allene Augusta Williams
Selma Carolyn Williams

Elizabeth EvalenaNickens

1946 Commencement Program
(555-179)

Douglas High School graduating class of 1947. Front row, left to right: Margaretta Virginia Gaither, Bernice Ford, Faye Johnson, second row, left to right: Audrey Harris, Arthur Gaither (valedictorian), Edward Bartlett (salutatorian), Colleen Jackson. (555-53).

Valedictory Address - given by Arthur Gaither 1947

Mr. Quarles, Teachers, Classmates, Parents and Friends

I, having been honored by being chosen to be valedictorian of the class of 1947, do take this occasion to say unto you in their behalf, the words of farewell.

Draw near, all of you, who have been friends of this most illustrious of all high school classes, and listen to these last words for, like all departing spirits, we have much to say in the last fleeting moments of our high school life.

Truly, indeed, do we believe, heart and soul, in the motto which we have chosen: "Life is Accomplishment, not mere Existence."

With this belief in ourselves, we step as a class across the boundary that separates school life from life's school. Feeling no fear of the great future, but inspired by our motto, we are certain of success so long as we are resolved upon every occasion to improve every opportunity for service and offer the world nothing less than our very best efforts.

Parents and friends, we extend our sincere thanks for all the privileges you have made possible for us to enjoy here. To all of you who have come to listen to us, we must voice our thanks for your attendance and warm appreciation you have given to our humble efforts to entertain you.

And now to you, dear faithful teachers, we, the graduating class which is about to pass through the doors of Douglas School, thank you with our last breath, for all that you have done for every part of us during the years we have been in your care. You have all had your part in instructing us. But we feel that you have also been very active in constructing us. You have all had a hand in our education. You have been, likewise, vital inspiration.

What is there left for our breaking hearts to say, as we face this last scene? But we thank you again, and may the blessing of God be upon you, in the hope that you will hold us, we beg of you, dear in memory.

Douglas High School graduating class of 1948. Left to right: Ann Cooke, Evelyn Lewis, Wallace Ford, Orissa Taper. (555-54)

Douglas High School graduating class of 1949. Front row, left to right: Rosa Gaither, Clifford Brooks Jr, Susie Johnson, Elsie Ford, Richard Ford Jr, Sarah Lewis; second row, left to right: Frances Williams, Mary Fisher, William Brown Jr, Adrian Emerson Cook, Milbert Taper, Meta Lee Turner; 3rd row, left to right: Margaret Cooke, Kirk Gaskins Jr., Joy A. Gaskins. (555-55)

Douglas High School graduating class of 1950. Front row, left to right, seated: Rosalie Bartlett, Nina Nickens, Jean Alexander; second row, left to right, standing: Kirk N. Gaskins (principal), Charles Burks, Harry Brown, Celesta Carter, Henry Bartlett, Effie McKinney (senior class advisor.) (618-25)

Douglas High School graduating class of 1951. Front row, left to right: Lois Wanzer (standing), Elizabeth Kreamer, Margaret Williams, June Gaskins (valedictorian), Ann Ford, Evelyn Brown, Alma Kane (standing), second row, left to right: Monroe Johnson, James Walden, Paul Burns, Roy Rhodes, Kenneth Carter. (555-57)

Douglas High School graduating class of 1952. Front row, left to right: Helen Rhodes, Shirley Hall, Charles H. Jackson (valedictorian), Gloria Finley, Bessie Dokes, Effie McKinney (senior class advisor); second row, left to right: Kirk Nathaniel Gaskins, Sr. (principal), Richard Pope, Edward Curry, Eva Marshall, Joan Elliott, Kenneth Cooke (salutatorian), Gilbert Caulk.
(555-58A)

Class of 1953

NO GRADUATING CLASS,
BECAUSE CURRICULUM WAS
EXTENDED THROUGH
TWELTH GRADE.

Douglas High School graduating class of 1954, first twelfth grade class. Front row, left to right: Shirley Bartlett, Charles Brown, Joan Brown, Andrew Gaskins (salutatorian), Barbara Turner (valedictorian); second row, left to right: Effie McKinney (senior class advisor), Walter Nickens, Jean Dyer, John Carter Finley, Kirk Nathaniel Gaskins, Sr (principal.) (555-59)

Baccalaureate sermon on June 6 by Rev. L.E. Terrell (not in photo), President, Storer College, Harpers Ferry, West Virginia. The class gift to the school was a new flag pole.

Douglas High School graduating class of 1955. Front row, left to right: Janet Lewis, Marlene Johnson (salutatorian), James Prather, Audrey Curry, Zita Laws, (valedictorian); second row, left to right: Hubert Stephenson, Anna Carter, Emma Henderson, Dabney Stephenson, Loretta Moten, Jean Allen, Michael Ford. (555-9)

Douglas High School graduating class of 1956. Front row, left to right: Floyd Burks, Gilbert Carter, David Clinton, Beverly Ann Long, Alexander Thomas, Helena Carter, Kirk N. Gaskins Sr. (principal); second row, left to right: Effie McKinney Davis (senior class advisor), Mildred Williams, Shirley Shields, James Bartlett, Beverly Gaskins, James Nickens, Cecelia Williams, Barbara Pye; third row, left to right: Audrey Wills, Elizabeth Jackson (valedictorian) Rebecca Robinson. (555-39)

Douglas High School graduating class of 1957. Front row, left to right: Shirley Dyer, Hattie Christian, Charles Walker, Carrie Gant (salutatorian), Grace Evans; second row, left to right: Annie Shields, James Carter, Sylvia Stephenson, James Stephenson, Janice Williams (valedictorian), James Finley, Maggie Burks. (555-61)

Douglas High School graduating class of 1958. Front row, left to right: Mrs. Effie McKinney Davis (senior class advisor), Margaret Jackson, Beverly Sue Harris (salutatorian), Elaine Parks, Josephine Gant, Inez Strother, Mr. Kirk N. Gaskins Sr (principal); second row, left to right: James Nelson, Thomas Washington, Shepherd Harris Jr, John Randolph Carter, John Benjamin Brown, Jr. (valedictorian); third row, left to right: John Spencer, Stephen Newman. (555-36)

Commencement Exercises will open with the Baccalaureate Sermon on Sunday at the school beginning at 8:30 p.m. The Rev. Charles A. Jones, pastor of St. Paul AME Church will deliver the sermon to the graduates. Graduation exercises will be held on June 6 at the school beginning at 8:30 p.m.

Certificate of Award

Presented to

James Elwood Walker

upon recommendation of the faculty of

Douglas High School

for outstanding accomplishment in

Football, Basketball

Given at *Douglas High School*

this *3* day of *June* A.D. 19*58*

Edwin L. Barksdale
Coach

K. N. Gaskins
Prin

James Elwood Walker graduated from Douglas High School, June 1959. He received a Certificate of Award for outstanding achievement in football and basketball. (555-151b)

Douglas High School graduating class of 1959. Front row seated, left to right: Sylvia Washington, Joseph Nickens, Brenda Bundy, Marshall Nickens, Anna Strother. second row, left to right: Kenneth Burks, Ann Ransom (salutatorian), Joy Ann Gaskins, James Walker, Edna Allen, Imogene Brown, Garland Williams; third row, left to right: Jack Brown (valedictorian), Katherine Gaither, Albert Delany Long, Judith Gaither, Augustus Gaskins Jr. (555-43)

The Douglas High School Band participated in commencement exercises for the first time last night. Under the direction of Tuscan Jasper, the group played the processional and the recessional. Supt. of Schools, Garland R. Quarles, presented diplomas to the sixteen graduates.

Douglas High School graduating class of 1960. Front row, left to right: Frank Jackson, Wanda Clifford, Bushrod Harris, Barbara Williams, Clifford Lee Mason, Ellen Delores Dyer; second row, left to right: Effie McKinley Davis (senior class advisor) Harriet Washington (salutatorian), Carter Alsberry, Charles Corley, Nancy Davis, Louis Newman, Theodore Tolliver, Tonya Cartwright (valedictorian); Kirk N. Gaskins Sr. (principal) third row, left to right: Ronald Moten, Melvin Cooper, Frank Lavender. (555-38)

Douglas High School graduating class of 1961. Front row, seated, left to right: Dorothy Scott, Joyce Brown, Jacqueline Williams, Mary Frances Washington (valedictorian), Katherine Ford; second row, standing, left to right: Kirk N. Gaskins Sr. (principal), Lawrence E. Carter, Randolph Elzey Greene, Moses W. Long, James McL. Brown (salutatorian), Effie McKinney Davis (senior class advisor.) (555-63)

Douglas High School graduating class of 1962. Front row, seated, left to right: Christine Brooks, Sharon Williams, Karlene Washington, Patricia Tolliver, Virginia Walker, Carolyn Gaither; second row, standing, left to right: Kirk Nathaniel Gaskins Sr. (principal), Stanley Long, Charles B. Harris (valedictorian), Charles Washington, Laurence E. Gaskins (salutatorian), Richard Harris, Robert Cooper, John Henry Laws, Jr., Effie McKinney Davis (senior class advisor.) (555-37A)

Douglas High School graduating class of 1963. Front row, left to right: Mary Brown, Joseph Kenneth Willis, Closia Gene King, Louis Long Jr., Maxine Blowe, George Curry Jr., Julia Brown, Paul Walker; second row, left to right: Effie McKinney Davis (senior class advisor), Faye Long (valedictorian), Phylis Veney, Donna Dixon; third row, left to right: Leroy Woodson, Jr., George Anthony, John Alsberry, Robert Newman, Paul Williams, Joseph Shields, Lucien Bannister Jr., Herman Jackson III, Charles W. Finley (salutatorian.) (555-44)

Commencement Exercises

Douglas High School

Winchester, Virginia

Tuesday evening, June 11, 1963

8:30 P. M.

Theme: Living For Tomorrow

PROGRAM

Processional

Invocation

Selections .... Glee Club

O Sing Ye To The Lord - Pitoni
Paper Reeds By The Brook - Thompson

Salutatorian ... "Staking Our Claim" ... Charles William Finley

Oration .... George Irvin Anthony

"On The Youth of Today Rests the Democracy of Tomorrow"

Oration ... "Divine Guidance and Inspiration" . Maxzine Blowe

Solo .... "I Walk With God" .... Lucien Bannister

Oration .... Paul David Williams

"Preparedness is the First Step Toward Success" (Motto)

Valedictorian ... "Living For Tomorrow" ... Faye Evelyn Long

Selection .... Glee Club

"Go Song of Mine" - Cookson

Presentation of Diplomas .... Supt. Garland R. Quarles

Recessional

Benediction

Industrial Arts Exhibit in Gymnasium

Douglas High School graduating class of 1964. Front row, left to right: Noah A. Laws, Georgia M. Cain, Elizabeth Moten, Sheila D. Humbert, Allen Carter; second row, left to right: Effie McKinney Davis (senior class advisor), Violet Blowe, Robin Washington, Charlena Washington (valedictorian), Betty J. Payne, Virginia Ann Washington, Priscilla Rodgers, Frances Carter (salutatorian), Kirk N. Gaskins, Sr. (principal.) (555-64)

Commonwealth of Virginia
Department of Education

This diploma is awarded to

Charlena Marie Washington

who has completed the requirements
for graduation from

Douglas High School

Given at Winchester, Virginia, this 10th day of June, 1964

Kirk N. Gaskins
Principal

Harland N. Quarles
Superintendent of Schools

Hulett H. Solenberger
Chairman of School Board

VALEDICTORIAN – Civic Responsibility
By Charlene Marie Washington Class of 1964

Dr. Quarles, Mr. Gaskins, Members of the faculty, and friends:

The Blue and White Spirit in Our lives has incorporated in it the principles that endow one with the qualities of civic responsibility. Our school is like a city in its organization. Each pupil fells the responsibility for the duties he is to perform. In the halls we acquire the courtesy and tat that make us share the responsibility for safety on the great highways. In the election of our school officers we assume a major civic duty to benefit the school. We elect superior leaders because we are zealous for attainment by our class.

In life, again we want to elect qualified officers to lead us and to preserve for us the glory and the freedom of our democracy. The principles of our spirit make us want to respect observance of school and civic laws. These lead us on to want to work together for the betterment of our school and the community. It offers encouragement and pushes us on to accomplish the goal of civic responsibility. It is our privilege, as true Americans to make use of our opportunity, to raise our standards of democracy higher and keep that torch forever burning for greater peace and happiness.

Friends, the time is here when we must bid farewell to the school, and members of the faculty. We shall, no doubt, come in contact with them after graduation, but there can never be that same feeling of unity which we have felt during our high school years. It is rather hard to say farewell to these outstanding influences in our lives. But we have a new beginning ahead of us, new roads to travel. There will be new fields to endeavor for each of us, whether they be in institutions of higher learning, in homes, or in the world of business.

To you, our parents, relatives, and friends, we express our gratitude, realizing that a mere "thank you" cannot repay this debt; and hope that we shall always merit the confidence you have had in us.

Classmates, this Spirit has meant to us Self-realization, Proper human relationships, learning the practices of economic efficiency, and actual civic responsibility.

Let us remember that no man liveth to himself alone. We are in a world of complex currents which make us mutually dependent. We cannot thrive but by the patronage of our neighbors; we cannot win but by their confidence and favor, which we cannot hold if we don't not serve them in turn.

We are starting up the slope of life. It is a beautiful way, for we are facing the sun, and the shadows fall behind us. It is a joyous way, even though there be stones to bruise our feet and thorns to prick our hands, for hope makes the heart sing though the eyes may weep.

We know that such a meeting as this will never be possible again, but we shall always be bound together by the intangible Blue and White Spirit. This is the one thing we have in common, and it will always serve as a bond, and a beacon light to guide us onward and upward.

As we have striven to live up to the standards, and have come thus far along the way, we have only finished this stage in our progress toward the goal, but we have also laid the foundation for future attainments as we go forth to accomplish new and greater achievements in our future lives.

Farewell friends.

Douglas High School graduating class of 1965. Front row, left to right: Joseph Cooke Jr (valedictorian), Mary Helen Harris (salutatorian), Judy Humbert, Harmon G. Byrd Jr, Diane Long, Osceola Shields, Alexander Finley; second row, left to right: Kirk Nathaniel Gaskins, Sr. (principal), Bernice Gant, Herman Grimes, Linda Long, Effie McKinney Davis (senior class advisor.) (555-65)

The Douglas School class of 1966, was the last class to graduate from the school. Front row, left to right: Augustine Lavender, Phyllis Nelson, Phyllis Washington (valedictorian), Lavenia Jackson (salutatorian), Gretchen Weaver; second row, left to right: Kirk N. Gaskins, Sr. (principal), Wayne King, Irvin Baltimore, Randolph Martin, Ronald Nelson, Effie McKinney Davis (senior class advisor.) (555-66)

COMMENCEMENT PROGRAM

Wednesday Evening, June 8th 1966
8:30 P. M.

THEME: A World of Peace and Security

Processional.................................... Audience Standing

Invocation

Selection.................................... Glee Club
"Oh, Holy Lord"   *Arranged by Hall Johnson*

Salutatorian........................... Lavenia Elizabeth Jackson

Oration...................................Randolph Nelson Martin

Selection.................................... Glee Club
"Jesu Joy of Man's Desiring"   *J. S. Bach*

Oration................................... Phyliss Jean Nelson

Valedictorian.....................Phyllis Jean Washington

Selection.................................... Glee Club
"Trust"   *J. Sibelius*

Presentation of Diplomas............. Supt., J. L. Johnson

Presentation of Awards

Alma Mater..................Audience Standing and Singing

Recessional

Benediction

~~Industrial Arts and Home Economics Exhibition
in Gymnasium~~

(555-176)

Nine Graduate From Douglas, Others Tonight

"The nine seniors at Douglas High School graduated last night, in the final commencement at that school.

Handley, Clarke County and Johnson-Williams High schools will have their graduation exercises tonight. James Wood will have its commencement tomorrow night.

The valedictory address at Douglas was given by Phyllis Jean Washington and the salutatory by Lavinia Jackson. Randolph Martin was the third honor student and Phyllis Jean Nelson, fourth.
Miss Washington received the Sanitary Dairy award for $100 and also a subscription to the Readers Digest.
Gretchen Weaver received the Good Citizenship award.
These awards were presented by Mrs. Effie M. Davis, senior advisor.
Mrs. Lovelena Marcus, homemaking instructor, presented the senior homemaking trophy to Miss Washington and the junior trophy to Helen Williams. The Home-Ec pin went to Lavinia Jackson.
The varsity basketball team presented a plaque to Coach Edwin Barksdale and a silver tray was given to Mrs. Marcus for her 39 years of service.
The Winchester Evening Star Athletic Award went to William Beamer and Robert Baltimore.
Theme of commencement program was "A World of Peace and Security."
Douglas school will close for good tomorrow. It will reopen in the fall as the Winchester Intermediate School for sixth and seventh graders. George L. Craig, Jr. will be the principal."

Winchester Evening Star
June 18, 1966

Winchester Evening Star

Prof P.W. Gibson principal of the Colored Schools in Winchester announces that the schools of the city and of Frederick County will hold the annual fair in the Douglas School in Winchester on Tuesday June 11 from 9:00 o'clock in the morning until 6 o'clock that afternoon. The closing exercise of the Douglas School will be held at the Mt. Carmel Baptist Church on Tuesday evening at 8:30 o'clock.

Winchester Evening Star
June 10, 1918

The Commencement Exercises will be held in the auditorium June 15th at 9:00 p.m. The program included 7th Grade honor Students recitation – *Our Childhood's School* – Orissa Taper, *The Lonely Clock* - Barbara Poulson. The salutatory address was given by Lorraine Turner and the valedictory address by Zelma Pinkett. Taylor Finley recited the *Twentieth Century Rubicon*. The commencement address was given by Rev. Clarence Davis and the Glee Club rendered several selections. These students received special awards and honors during the year: first, second and thirds prizes for best scrap books illustrating the five fields in our World of Work were awarded to Wesley Alsberry, Velonda Deneal and Helena Pines. Home Economics students doing outstanding work for the year were Wesley Alsberry, Velonda Deneal, Helena Pines, Charlotte Shields, June Banks, Bernice Ford and Alice Crawford.

Winchester Evening Star
June 14, 1944

The Faculty has just released the names of all the prospective seventh and the eleventh grades. Seventh graders include: Beulah Bannister, Elenora Cary, Elsie Ford, Rosa Gaither, Joyce Gaskins, Mary Jackson, Sarah Lewis, Milbert Taper, Meta Turner, Clifford Brooks, William Brown, Celesta Carter, Emerson Cook, Floyd Finley, Richard Ford, Kirk Gaskins Jr., and Madison Walker. Below are the nine members of the Senior class arranged according to class standing: Anna Wanzer, Valedictorian, Lanier Turner, Salutatorian, Mary Wanzer, Mary Mitchell, Alberta Washington, Alice Crawford, Lewis Gaither, Vivian Taper, and Ellen Williams.

Winchester Evening Star
May 4, 1945

A very inspiring sermon was given to the graduates on Sunday, June 3 by Rev. J. Dallas Jenkins of Luray. His text was, "Behold I send you forth as sheep in the midst of wolves, be ye therefore wise as serpents and harmless as doves." His subject, "Meeting Life."

Winchester Evening Star
June 6, 1945

Douglas School has announced its Commencement activities. Baccalaureate exercises will be held in the Douglas School auditorium Sunday, June 2, 1946 at 8:30 p.m. Rev. Alexander Early, Principal of the Williams Training School, Berryville, Virginia will deliver the sermon to the seniors. Certificates will be awarded to seventh grade graduates: Rosalie Bartlett, Helen Blowe, Gladys Brooks, Gladys Cary, Doris Catlett, Margaret Donnelly, Jane Ethel Johnson, Helen Robinson, Sadie Washington, Henry Bartlett, William Bannister, Harry Brown, Robert Cook, John Fetus, Lowell Poulson, and Roy Rhodes.

Winchester Evening Star
May 21, 1946

The Douglas High School will graduate five at commencement exercises to be held Thursday, June 6, at 8:30 p.m. Diplomas will be presented by Garland R. Quarles, city school superintendent. Class members include: Sue Catlett (valedictorian), Selma Williams (salutatorian), Josephine Catlett, Allene Williams and Elizabeth Nickens. The high school glee club will sing three selections, *The Heavens Resound, Waiting in the Shadows, Tramp Tramp, Tramp*. Invocation at the exercises will be delivered by the Rev. A. T. Gaskins.

Winchester Evening Star
June 4, 1946

The senior class stood on pins awaiting the verdict as to who would be in the line of march on June 9. Recently they came to a standstill to accept the following candidates for graduation: Charles Jackson (valedictorian), Kenneth Cook (salutatorian), Shirley Hall, Joan Elliott, Eva Marshall, Gloria Finley, Richard Pope, Helen Rhoades, Gilbert Caulk, Edward Curry and Bessie Dokes.

Winchester Evening Star
May 9, 1952

Baccalaureate Services will be held at the Douglas School Auditorium on Sunday, evening, June 8, 8:30 o'clock. The address will be made by the Rev. Julius S. Carroll, pastor of the John Mann M. E. Church. Commencement exercises at Douglas High School will be held on June 9, at 8:30 o'clock. The exercises will be followed by exhibits in the Industrial Arts Shop and Home Economics Room 3.

Winchester Evening Star
June 2, 1952

Diplomas were awarded to the eight member senior class at the Douglas High School last night. The class gift to the school was a new flag pole. Andrew Gaskins received the awards for leadership and was also named honor student. Barbara Turner received a leadership award. An award for leadership and athletic activities was presented to Shirley Bartlett. John Finley received the Winchester Lions Club music award.

Winchester Evening Star
June 8, 1954

Two of Douglas High School's top athletes, James Prather and Michael Ford, have been awarded athletic scholarships to Elizabeth City State Teachers College, Elizabeth City, North Carolina. The scholarships each worth $425.00 were awarded the lads because of their excellence in football.

Winchester Evening Star
June 11, 1955

Douglas Alumni Association

Douglas Alumni Association

According to minutes of early meetings, the Douglas Alumni Association was formed in 1934 under the direction of Dr. Taylor Floyd Finley. This was confirmed by President F. Ellsworth Turner's comments to the board of governors at a meeting in 1972. A *Winchester Evening Star* article dated July 11, 1938, shows that a meeting of the Alumni Association would be held in the school auditorium. All graduates of the school and other members of the association were invited to attend as matters pertaining to projects for the coming year would be discussed. Officers listed were: F. Ellsworth Turner, President Mrs. Frances Finley Moten, Secretary; and Mrs. Wallace (Katherine) Shelton Ford, Treasurer.

The Douglas Alumni Association published an article in the *Winchester Evening Star* (March 28, 1940) indicating that the 1940 drive for funds would be opened on March 28 and would extend through April 11. Charles C. Reed would serve as Chairman. Members were urged to keep the campaign in mind and were assured that all gifts of any size would be greatly appreciated.

An announcement in the *Winchester Evening Star* dated September 21, 1946, showed a meeting of the association that evening at 8:30 pm at 803 S. Cameron Street. F. Ellsworth Turner continued as president, Mrs. Frances Moten as Secretary and Dr. Taylor F. Finley as Coordinator. Members living in Philadelphia, New York, Boston,

Dr. Taylor Floyd Finley (Class of 1918), a Winchester dentist and former Douglas teacher, founded the Douglas Alumni Association in 1934.(204-65 thl)

Harrisburg, Baltimore and Washington, DC were expected to attend.

The Douglas Alumni Association has continued to meet over the years and has journeyed to Washington, D.C. and to King William, Virginia, for annual meetings hosted by members. For many years the meetings and dinners were held at Tokes Inn in Opequon, Virginia.

On September 11, 1971, Mrs. Sharon Williams Harris asked the Board of Governors of the Douglas Alumni Association to consider establishing a scholarship fund to help a local high school graduate with college expenses. At a meeting on October 24, 1971, the board agreed to set up the Lovelena Lomax Scholarship Fund in honor of Mrs. Marcus and her forty (40) years of dedicated service. Mrs. Sharon Williams Harris was named Chairlady of the scholarship fund. The first early fund raisers were raffles and a food stand during the Apple Blossom Festival in 1976. Another successful fund raiser was the selling of tee shirts and sweat shirts with the school's picture on the front.

In May of 1977, specifications for the award were drawn up and presented to Handley High School officials. The initial terms indicated that the award was: "Established in

1977 by members of the Douglas Alumni Association in honor of teachers and students of Douglas School, the sum of $125.00 per year, for four (4) years will be given to help a deserving minority member graduate of Handley High School to continue his/her education at an accredited institution of higher learning. The recipient is to be chosen by the Handley Faculty Scholarship Committee based upon financial need, leadership, citizenship and scholarship. It is also requested that the student have a family member connected to Douglas, prior to the closing of the school in 1966. Payment will be made to the institution of higher learning in which the graduate has enrolled."

The first scholarship was presented in 1977 to Frances Whitacre by Mr. William Buckner. Mr. Buckner was then a member of the Winchester School Board. It was determined that when schedules permit, the previous year's winner would present the scholarship to the current year's recipient.

In 1986, the board agreed to increase the amount of the award to $1,000.00. At that time, it was also agreed to present a scholarship to a student from James Wood High School, (Winchester, Virginia,) Central High School (Woodstock, Virginia,) and to Strasburg High School, (Strasburg, Virginia). This was to honor the many students from Frederick and Shenandoah counties who rode school buses to Douglas each day to attend high school. The award for Frederick and Shenandoah counties was to be in the amount of $500.00 per school. The same principles applied as used at Handley, each school's scholarship selection committee will choose the recipient.

Currently, the scholarship distribution and amounts is as follows: City of Winchester, Virginia (Handley High School - $2000), Frederick County, Virginia (James Wood High School - $1000, Sherando High School -

$1000, and Millbrook High School - $1000), and Shenandoah County, Virginia (Central High School - $1000, and Strasburg High School - $1000). Records of the Douglas Alumni Association show that since the original scholarship was awarded in 1977 more than 70 students related to someone that attended Douglas School prior to 1966 have benefitted from the approximate $80,000 distributed in scholarships.

F. Ellsworth Turner, c. 2000, first president of the Douglas Alumni Association (555-106)

In addition to the scholarship program, the alumni association has been active throughout the community. During the 1980's, they worked with Dr. Warren Hofstra's history class at Shenandoah University in collecting oral history interviews of former Douglas students, conducted several oral interviews with old black citizens to document their recollection of local history and changes over time.

They collected photographs of local Afro Americans for a display at the library—one display on women of the community and an additionl display on local history items. The alumni association also recorded tombstones in Orrick cemetery and prepared a list of this information which was donated to the Stewart Bell Jr. Archives in the Handley Library.

They partnered with the Friends of the Handley Library and hosted a reception for civil rights icon Dr. James Farmer when he visited Handley Library March 27, 1986.

Members of the Alumni Association compiled a booklet for the children of former Douglas High School coach, Edwin K. Barksdale, highlighting sports at Douglas during his tenure with written tributes by former studends and athletes. In 1988, the association published a souvenir photo booklet of the attendees at the annual dinner and dance. During the early months of 1990, alumni association members collected signatures and presented a petition to the Winchester School Board to establish a school with the name of Frederick Douglass Elementary School opened in the fall of 1990. Working with the Winchester-Frederick County Historical Society, the association assisted in compiling information and submitting an application to have Douglas School on North Kent Street declared a Virginia Historical Landmark in September 19, 1999. It was placed on the National Register of Historical Places effective May 26, 2000.

Over the years on the first weekend of October, the association has held Douglas Weekend which consisted of a Meet and Greet on Friday evening and a dinner and dance on Saturday evening. This has since changed to a Meet and Greet held at the Douglas Community Learning Center (former Douglas School Building) on Saturday morning and a Black Tie Dinner/ Dance at various banquet facilities in Winchester on Saturday evening.

F. Ellsworth Turner, Class of 1931, served as President of the Douglas Alumni Association for 53 years (1935-1988) prior to turning over the reins of leadership to Sharon Williams Harris, Class of 1962, who currently maintains the position.

Winchester Evening Star

George Hogans, a captain at Rock Castle; Miss Zelma Pinkett and Miss June Banks who are attending Virginia State College visited our school recently. We are glad to hear that they are getting along nicely in college.

Winchester Evening Star
January 15, 1945

The faculty and student body were delighted to have Captain George Hogans of St. Emma Military School visit our school Tuesday while waiting to be inducted into the armed services.

Winchester Evening Star
March 2, 1945

Douglas School was recently visited by these former students: Lee Honesty in the Army, James Fisher in the Army and Lawrence Williams in the Navy.

Winchester Evening Star
October 12, 1945

We were honored with the presence of Sgt. Henry M. Brooks who spoke to the student body on his travels since serving with the U.S. Army. Sgt. Brooks highlighted with interest the events he experienced and souvenirs he collected from different countries.

Winchester Evening Star
November 17, 1945

F. Ellsworth Turner, president of the Douglas Alumni Association announced today that there will be a meeting tonight of all graduates of Douglas School at 8:30 p.m. The meeting will be held at 803 S. Cameron Street. Mrs. Frances Moten is secretary of the association and Dr. T. F. Finley is coordinator. Members who are living in Philadelphia, New York, Boston, Harrisburg, Baltimore and Washington, DC are expected to attend.

Winchester Evening Star
September 21, 1946

Many of our graduates have chosen Storer College, Harpers Ferry, W.Va,. as their institution of higher learning. Those attending the college are Josephine and Sue Catlett. The Catlett sisters are majoring in elementary education. Roland Harper, a graduate of l945, has returned to Storer to complete his senior year. Taylor Finley Jr. has entered his junior year to complete a pre-medical course. Among the many World War II veterans of Douglas who are taking advantage of the opportunities offered at Storer College are Reginald Mitchell and George Hogans.

Winchester Evening Star
October 4, 1946

Mrs. Hattie Mitchell Lea has retired from the Douglas School Alumni Association Council. To honor her, a banquet was held June 10 by the association at Tokes Inn. F. Ellsworth Turner, as president, was toast master. Invocation was given by Rev. D. E. Fields, pastor of St Paul AME church. Guest speaker for the evening was Dr. Sarah W. Brown, member of the board of trustees Howard University. Charles Tomas sang. Officers of the association besides Turner are: Mr. John Triplett, Mrs. Frances Hogans Lewis, Dr. T. F. Finley and Henry M. Brooks.

Winchester Evening Star
May 10, 1948

The following students are furthering their studies at Virginia State College, Ettrick, Virginia and Storer College, Harpers Ferry, West Virginia. Meta Turner has entered her sophomore year at Virginia State College. Miss Rosalie Bartlett has entered the Freshman Class at Storer College while her brother Edward is resuming studies in the sophomore Class at Virginia State College. Kirk Gaskins, Jr. left for Virginia State College last Monday to enter the Freshman Class and Clifford Brooks, Jr. began his second year in the same school.

Winchester Evening Star
October 3, 1950

Kirk N. Gaskins, Jr. of this city has recently been named to the Dean's List at Storer College, Harpers Ferry. This honor means that he has been on the Honor Roll for academic excellence throughout the semester.

Winchester Evening Star
March 2, 1952

Kirk N. Gaskins, Jr., a student at Storer College in Harpers Ferry, was chosen to be on the Dean's List for academic excellence during the final term of college. This announcement was made at the annual Honors Day held recently.

Winchester Evening Star
June 2, 1952

During the Thanksgiving holidays, many of our former graduates were home from college. They talked to many of us about their studies and college in general. Their talks were a great encouragement to many students who had decided to quit high school or forget the idea of college. Those students were Marlene Johnson attending St. Phillip's School of Nursing, James Prather and Charles Brown both from Maryland State College, and Dabney Stephenson and Vita Laws from Virginia State College.

Winchester Evening Star
December 3, 1955

Charles M. Brown, son of Mr. & Mrs. William H. Brown recently received his B.S. Degree in business education from Maryland State College, Division of University of Maryland at Princess Anne. Mr. Brown is reported to be one of the very few undergraduates in the country who has had an article published. With Dr. V. W. Stone, he wrote an article entitled *The Application of Mathematical Statistics To The Stock Market* which appeared in the February 5, 1959 issue of the *Commercial and Financial Chronicle*. Mr. Brown plans to teach business subjects on a secondary school level.

Winchester Evening Star
June 1, 1960

Charles M. Jackson, son of Mr. & Mrs. Herman Jackson, will be graduated Monday from Montana State College, Bozeman, Montana. At the same time, he will be commissioned in the U.S. Army at the annual Review and Awards Ceremony.

Winchester Evening Star
June 3, 1960

Edward D. Curry, son of Mr. & Mrs. Henry Curry, recently received his B.S. Degree from Maryland State Teacher's College at Bowie, Maryland. Mr. Curry plans to teach in Maryland and was an honor student during his junior and senior years.

Winchester Evening Star
June 15, 1960

James Farmer with Frances and William Buckner, March 26, 1987

James Farmer at his book signing, March 26, 1987

Elizabeth Washington, Charlena W. Childs, Calvin Gant, Sr., and James Farmer

Left to right: Rebecca Ebert, Jasper Long, Effie Davis, and James Farmer.

Betty Bannister and Ann Grogg at Douglas School celebration on April 24, 1990. (555-32)

Warren Hofstra and Garfield Prather at Douglas School celebration on April 24, 1990.

Floyd Finley III and Dr. John Capehart observing trophies at Frederick Douglas School celebration on April 24, 1990. (555-33)

Left to right: Sharon Harris, Judy Humbert, and Rebecca Ebert at Frederick Douglas School Celebration on April 24, 1990. (555-29)

Hester Harris and Mattie R. Cross, former teachers, at Douglas School celebration on April 24, 1990.

Sharon Harris at Douglas School celebration on April 24, 1990. Kathryn Shelton Ford, 1927 graduate and school cafeteria manager, in background. (555-28)

Shepherd Harris and Charles Corley with Judy Humbert at Douglas School celebration on April 24, 1990. (555-31)

Annual Douglas Alumni Dinner

UAW Building
2625 Paper Mill Road
Winchester, Virginia 22601

Saturday, October 7, 1995
7:00 P.M. - 1:00 A.M.
Price: $25.00 Per Person Dinner and Dance

Music By: WINCHESTER'S OWN "BASEMENT FUNK"

Sponsored By: Douglas Alumni Association
For The Scholarship Fund

Dinner Catered by Jesse Curry

21 and Over - BYOB

Virginia Historic Landmark plaque. (555-113a)

Douglas School Dedication Ceremony and Alumni Open House, October 2, 1999. Attendees: Patricia Finley, Ella Finley, Floyd Finley, Thomas T. Byrd (owner & publisher of *The Winchester Star.*) (1493-126)

Sharon and Charles Harris
2001

Displays of
school history
and
memorabilia at
Douglas
Alumni
Association
Meet and
Greet, 2003.
(555-116c)

F. Ellsworth Turner families. Pictured left to right: Gertrude Turner Wills, Joanna Wills, Lawrence Turner, Deborah Turner, Margaret Turner, William W. Turner, and Ruth W. Turner (1493-129 thl)

Three former Douglas School staff members at Douglas Alumni dinner dance, 2004. Rosalie Bartlett Barksdale (Mrs. Edwin K. Barksdale), office; Ethel Wilds Wheeler, English teacher; Shirley Bruton Callis, girls' physical education and chemistry.

Loretta Moten
Coates and
Earl H. Coates
Douglas
Alumni Dinner
Dance (1710-5
thl)

David Burks,
Dorothy Curry Finley
and Zellene Long
Glover Douglas
Alumni Dinner
Dance (1710-6 thl)

Alexander Thomas
and Beverly Long
Thomas Douglas
Alumni Dinner
Dance (1710-4 thl)

William and Cynthia Martin Banks Douglas Alumni Dance (1710-8 thl)

William Mason and
Karlene Washington
Mason (class of
1962) Douglas
Alumni Dinner
Dance (1710-7 thl)

June Gaskins Davis and Kirk N. Gaskins Jr., (555-07)

Margaret Cook Crawford, Adrian Emerson Cook, Joy Gaskins Jordan, William Brown Jr., Mary Fisher Washington, Floyd Finley, III., Kirk N. Gaskins, Jr.
(1493-128 THL)

Charles W. Finley
(1493-130 THL)

Beverly Long Thomas and Loretta Moten Coates (555-116F wfchs)

Appendix A
Scholarship Recipients, 1977-2013

1977	Frances Whitacre	Hampton University	$500.00
1978	Alton Ramey	University of Virginia	$500.00
1979	Sandy Williams	Shenandoah College	$500.00
1980	Charles Small	Hampden-Sydney	$500.00
1981	Nancy Lynn Finley	James Madison University	$500.00
1982	Candace Davenport	Virginia State College	
		Lord Fairfax Community College	$500.00
1983	Danielle Jackson	West Virginia University	$500.00
1984	Fara D. Greene	William and Mary College	$500.00
1985	Keysha D. Washington	Lord Fairfax Community College	$500.00
1986	Sonia Ford	Old Dominion University	$500.00
1987	Andria Humbert	Virginia Commonwealth University	$1,000.00
1988	Lisa S. Williams	Hampton Institute	$1,000.00
	Elandra Pendleton	Strasburg High School	
		Lord Fairfax Community College	$500.00
1989	Mary Walker	Handley High School	$1,000.00
	Nytasha Brisco	James Wood High School	
$500.00			
	Gerald Nickens	Strasburg High School	$500.00
1990	Shanta Summers	Handley High School	$1,000.00
	Melissa Turner	James Wood High School	$500.00
	Shirley DeNeal	Strasburg High School	$500.00
1991	Daimon Caulk	Handley High School	
		Virginia Commonwealth University	$1,000.00
	Annie Berger	James Wood High School	
		Lord Fairfax Community College	$500.00
1992			
1993	Renee Shields	Handley High School	$1,000.00
	Candace Nelson	James Wood High School	
		Virginia Commonwealth University	$500.00
1994			
1995	Tara Ford	Handley High School	$1,000.00
1996	Alecia Polston	Handley High School	
		Greensboro College	$1,000.00
1997	Leslie Mason	Handley High School	$1,500.00
	Natalie Byrd	James Wood High School	
		Virginia State University	$1,000.00
	Sean Burns	Sherando High School	$1,000.00
1998	Alecia Cain		$1,000.00
1999	Israel Brooks	Handley High School	
		Lord Fairfax Community College	$1,500.00
	Carolyn Christian	Sherando High School	
		Lord Fairfax Community College	$1,000.00
	Monica Strother	Strasburg High School	
		Virginia State University	$1,000.00
	Natasha M. Roberts	Strasburg High School	$1,000.00

2000	Melissa Williams	Handley High School	
		Lord Fairfax Community College	$1,500.00
	Stephanie Roberts	James Wood High School	$1,000.00
	Tavis Laws	SherandoHigh School	$1,000.00
2001	Jakkara Masi Long	Handley High School	
		Norfolk State University	$2,000.00
	Traci Day	James Wood High School	
		Concord College	$1,000.00
	Vincent Carter Jr.	Sherando High School	
		Lord Fairfax Community College	$1,000.00
	Kenneth Strother	Strasburg High School	
		Lord Fairfax Community College	$1,000.00
2002	Catherine Scott	Handley High School	
		George Mason University	$2,000.00
	Timeka Milton	Strasburg High School	
		Virginia Union University	$1,000.00
2003	Daly Russ	Handley High School	
		Campbell University	$2,000.00
	Garth D. Williams	Sherando High School	
		Lord Fairfax Community College	$1,000.00
	Torrence J. Temple	Strasburg High School	
		Lord Fairfax Community College	$1,000.00
2004	Jocelyn R. Coates	Handley High School	
		Lord Fairfax Community College	$2,000.00
	Maxmillian Brisco	Sherando High School	
		Lord Fairfax Community College	$1,000.00
	Jamie A. Brown	Strasburg High School	
		Shepherd University	$1,000.00
2005	Justin L. Williams	Handley High School	
		Lord Fairfax Community College	$2,000.00
	Francesca A. Walker-Daniell	Millbrook High School	
		Lord Fairfax Community College	$1,000.00
	Jessica Nicole Brown	Strasburg High School	
		Marymount University	$1,000.00
2006	Charles H. Washington	Handley High School	
		Christopher Newport University	$2,000.00
	Douglas W. Jackson Jr.	Sherando High School	
		Shepherd University	$1,000.00
2007	Justin Michael Mason	Handley High School	
		James Madison University	$2,000.00
	Lindsay Marie Carter	Sherando High School	
		James Madison University	$1,000.00
	Cassandra Leigh Williams	Strasburg High School	
		Old Dominion University	$1,000.00
	Nykeya Mathes	Millbrook High School	
		Lord Fairfax Community College	$1,000.00

2008	Rachel Allison Lavender	Handley High School Christopher Newport University	$2,000.00
	Daniel T. Grimes	Millbrook High School University of Virginia	$1,000.00
2009	Vance Beamer Washington	Handley High School Old Dominion University	$2,000.00
	Lauren Michelle Carter	Sherando High School University of Virginia	$1,000.00
	Mason Alsberry	Strasburg High School Radford University	$1,000.00
2010	Baxter Newman	Sherando High School Lord Fairfax Community College	$1,000.00
	Kara M. Dixon	Handley High School University of Maryland	$2,000.00
	Emily Ann Long	Millbrook High School Virginia Union University	$1,000.00
2011	Adrienne Jackson	Handley High School Old Dominion University	$2,000.00
2012	Shatara Butler	Handley High School Lord Fairfax Community College	$2,000.00
	Donte Harris	Millbrook High School Eastern Mennonite University	$1,000.00
	Devon Newman	Sherando High School Hagerstown Junior College	$1,000.00
	Corissa Alsberry	Strasburg High School	$1,000.00
2013	Darion Robinson	Handley High School Radford University (?)	$2,000.00
	Shaneece Mathes	Millbrook High School Lord Fairfax Community College	$1,000.00
	Darian Banks	Sherando High School George Mason University	$1,000.00
2014	Alexsis Thompson	Handley High School Radford University	$2,000.00
	Isaiah Williams	Sherando High School Potomac State College	$1,000.00
			$82,500.00

Appendix B
Douglas Faculty Roster 1919-1966

Year	Teacher	Enrollment	Notes
1919-1920	Powell W. Gibson – Principal Lena Barnett Hattie Mitchell William Smith – Janitor		
1920-1921	Same as above	Enrollment 161	
1921-1922	Same as above	Enrollment 180	
1922-1923	Same as above		
1923-1924	Powell W. Gibson – Principal Lena Barnett Anna Quiett Brooks Hattie Mitchell William Smith – Janitor	Enrollment	
1924-1925	Same as above	Enrollment 183	
1925-1926	Same as above	Enrollment 174	
1926-1927	Powell W. Gibson - Principal Lena Barnett Anna Quiett Brooks Hattie Mitchell William Smith – Janitor Elizabeth Thompson	Enrollment 209	In October of 1926 an agreement was made with Mt. Carmel Baptist Church to rent their basement for 8 months - $20.00 per month to handle the overflow of students.
1927-1928	Powell W. Gibson – Principal Anna Quiett Brooks Lovelena Lomax William Marcus Hattie Mitchell William Smith – Janitor Elizabeth Thompson	Enrollment 208	
1928-1929	Same as above	Enrollment 208	
1929-1930	Powell W. Gibson – Principal Anna Quiett Brooks Taylor Finley Lovelena Lomax William Marcus Hattie Mitchell William Smith – Janitor Elizabeth Thompson	Enrollment 189	
1930-1931	Powell W. Gibson - Principal Anna Quiett Brooks Taylor Finley Lovelena Lomax Hattie Mithell William Smith - Janitor	Enrollment 208	

Year	Teacher	Enrollment	Notes
1931-1932	Powell W. Gibson - Principal Taylor Finley Hattie Mithell Lea Lovelena L. Marcus	Enrollment 209	
1932-1933	Powell W. Gibson - Principal Marie B. Briscoe Taylor F. Finley Hattie M. Lea Lovelena L. Marcus Anna Brooks Tokes	Enrollment 216	
1933-1934	Same as above	Enrollment 210	
1934-1935	Same as above	Enrollment 232	Federal Government gave states money to inroduce adult education classes
1935-1936	Same as above	Enrollment 196	
1936-1937	Same as above	Enrollment 223	
1937-1938	Same as above	Enrollment 217	
1938-1939	Powell W. Gibson - Principal Kirk N. Gaskins Sr. - Jr. High Hattie M. Lea - 2nd & 3rd Lovelena L. Marcus - Jr. High Anna Q. Tokes - 4th & 5th Nerissa T. Wright - 1st	Enrollment 209	
1939-1940	Powell W. Gibson - Principal Simon Cook Kirk N. Gaskins Sr. Hattie M. Lea Lovelena L. Marcus Blanche G. Moten Anna Q. Tokes Nerissa T. Wright	Enrollment 241	
1940-1941	Kirk N. Gaskins Sr. - Principal Simon Cook Roy Dendy - Janitor Francis M. Jackson Hattie M. Lea Lovelena L. Marcus Blanche G. Moten Anna Q. Tokes Sterling Walker Nerissa T. Wright	Enrollment 253	
1941-1942	Kirk N. Gaskins Sr. - Principal Roy Dendy - Janitor Thomas Haywood - HS &Industrial Arts Francis M. Jackson - 7th & HS Hattie M. Lea - 2nd & 3rd Lovelena L. Marcus - 7th & HS Blanche G. Moten - 3rd & 4th Anna Q. Tokes - 5th & 6th Sterling W. Walker - HS Nerissa T. Wright - 1st	Enrollment 242	

Year	Teacher	Enrollment	Notes
1943-1944	Kirk N. Gaskins Sr. - Principal & HS Roy Dendy - Janitor Francis M. Jackson - 7th & HS Alma L. Layton - 1st Hattie M. Lea - 2nd & 3rd Lovelena L. Marcus - 7th & Home Ec. Blanches G. Moten - 3rd & 4th Effie McKinney - HS Anna Q. Tokes - 5th & 6th Nerissa T. Wright - 7th	Enrollment 211	
1944-1945	Kirk N. Gaskins Sr. - Principal & 11th Roy Dendy - Janitor Francis M. Jackson - 10th Alma L. Layton - 1st & 2nd Hattie M. Lea - 3rd & 4th Lovelena L. Marcus - 9th Effie McKinney - 8th Blanche G. Moten - 2nd & 3rd Anna Q. Tokes - 5th & 6th Nerissa T. Wright - 7th	Enrollment 213	
1945-1946	Kirk N. Gaskins Sr. - Principal & HS Clarence Davis - HS Roy Dendy - Janitor Francis M. Jackson - 7th & HS Alma L. Layton - 1st Hattie M. Lea - 2nd & 3rd Lovelena L. Marcus - 7th & Home Ec. Blanches G. Moten - 3rd & 4th Effie McKinney - HS Anna Q. Tokes - 5th Nerissa T. Wright - 6th	Enrollment 214	
1946-1947	Kirk N. Gaskins Sr. - Principal & HS math Clarence Davis - Industrial Arts Roy Dendy - Janitor Francis M. Jackson - HS English & History Alma L. Layton - 1st Hattie M. Lea - 3rd & 4th Lovelena L. Marcus - 7th & Home Ec Effie M. McKinney - HS Science Blanche G. Moten - 2nd Anna Q. Tokes - 5th Margaret L. Washington - 6th	Enrollment 221	
1947-1948	Kirk N. Gaskins Sr. - Principal & 11th Rev. Clarence Davis - 9th Roy Dendy - Janitor Francis M. Jackson - 10th Alma L. Layton - 1st Hattie M. Lea - 3rd & 4th Lovelena L. Marcus - 7th. Effie McKinney - 8th Blance G. Moten - 2nd & 3rd Anna Q. Tokes - 5th Margaree Washington - 6th	Enrollment 233	

Year	Teacher	Enrollment	Notes
1948-1949	Kirk N. Gaskins Sr. - Principal & 11th Charles Dendy - 9th Roy Dendy - Janitor Francis M. Jackson - 10th Alma L. Layton - 1st Lovelena L. Marcus - 7th Effie McKinney - 8th Blanches G. Moten - 2nd & 3rd Mattie Russell - 3rd & 4th Anna Q. Tokes - 5th Margaree Washington - 6th	Enrollment 243	
1949-1950	Kirk N. Gaskins Sr. - Principal & 11th Charles Dendy - 10th & Industrial Arts Francis M. Jackson - 11th Alma L. Layton - 1st Lovelena L. Marcus - 8th Effie M. McKinney - 8th Blanche G. Moten - 2nd & 3rd Mattie Russell - 4th & 5th Anna Q. Tokes - 5th Margaree Washington - 7th	Enrollment 247	
1950-1951	Kirk N. Gaskins Sr. - Principal Edwin K. Barksdale - 9th C. Dendy - 11th Roy Dendy - Janitor Francis M. Jackson - 11th Alma L. Layton - 1st Lovelena M. Marcus - 8th Effie McKinney - 12th Blanches G. Moten - 2nd & 3rd Mrs. Pegram - Librarian & Typing Mattie Russell - 4th & 5th Anna Q. Tokes - 5th & 6th Mrs. Washington	Enrollment 211	Tuition $170.00
1951-1952	Kirk N. Gaskins Sr. - Principal Roy Dendy - Janitor Norris Oliver Hite - 8th & P.E. Francis M. Jackson - 10th Alva Johnson - Janitor Francis M. Jackson Miss Mildred E. Leigh - Business teacher Lovelena L. Marcus -9th Effie M. McKinney - 11th Blanche G. Moten - 2nd & 3rd Mattie Russell - 3rd & 4th Anna Q. Tokes - 5th & 6th Mrs. Irene Wallace - Librarian Margaret L. Washington - 6th & 7th	Enrollment 275	Tuition $220.00

Year	Teacher	Enrollment	Notes
1952-1953	Kirk N. Gaskins Sr. - Principal Edwin K. Barksdale - 9th, P.E./Coach Charles Dendy - 8th Roy Dendy - Janitor Hester Harris - 1st Francis M. Jackson - 10th Alva Johnson - Janitor Lovelena L. Marcus - 9th Effie M. McKinney - 11th Blanche G. Moten - 2nd & 3rd Mattie Russell - 3rd & 4th Mildred Leigh Shriver - Business Teacher Anna Q. Tokes - 5th & 6th Irene Wallace - Librarian Margaree Washington - 7th	Enrollment 262	
1953-1954	Kirk N. Gaskins Sr. - Principal Edwin K. Barksdale - 8th Ruth Barksdale - 8th Charles Dendy - 9th Gloria Dendy - clerk Roy Dendy - Janitor Hester Harris - 1st Alva Johnson - Janitor Francis M. Jackson - 11th Lovelena L. Marcus - 9th Effie McKinney - 12th Dorothy Moorman 0 10th/Commercial Teacher Blanche G. Moten - 2nd & 3rd Mattie Russell - 3rd & 4th Anna Q. Tokes - 5th & 6th Irene Wallace - Librarian Margaree Washington - 7th	Enrollment 281	Tuition $250.00
1954-1955	Same as above with exceptions below Effie M. Davis (formally McKinney) Anna Tokes retired June, 1955 after 31 years of service.	Enrollment 289	Tuition $235.00
1955-1956	Kirk N. Gaskins Sr. - Principal Edwin K. Barksdale - 8th, 9th, 10th, P.E., Coach Ruth Barksdale - 11th Mary L. Byrd - Migrant Program Effie M. Davis - 12th Charles Dendy - 8th Gloria Dendy - Clerk Roy Dendy - Janitor Hester Harris - 1st Francis M. Jackson - 10th Tuscan Jasper - 9th & 10th Alva Johnson - Janitor Lovelena L. Marcus - 9th Dorothy Moorman -8th Blanche G. Moten - 2nd & 3rd Mattie Russell - 3rd & 4th Irene Wallace - Librarian Margaree Washington - 7th Margaret Williams - 6th & 7th	Enrollment 305	Tuition $270.00

Year	Teacher	Enrollment	Notes
1956-1957	Kirk N. Gaskins Sr. - Principal Edwin K. Barksdale - 9th Ruth Barksdale - 11th Henry M. Brooks - 8th Mary Byrd - Migrant program Mattie M. Cross - 3rd & 4th Mary J. Dandridge - 8th Effie M. Davis - 12th Hester Harris - 1st Carrie E. Hines - Librarian Francis M. Jackson - 10th Tuscan Jasper - 8th, 9th, 10th Alva Johnson - Janitor Lovelena L. Marcus - 9th Blanche G. Moten - 2nd & 3rd Loretta Moten - Clerk Iona B. Robinson - Substitute Margaree Washington - 6th & 7th Margaret Williams - 5th & 6th	Enrollment 317	Tuition $280.00
1957-1958	Kirk N. Gaskins Sr. - Principal Edwin K. Barksdale - 9th Ruth Barksdale - 11th Henry M. Brooks - 8th Mary L. Byrd - Migrant program Mattie R. Cross Effie M. Davis - 12th Mary J. Dandridge - 8th Hester Harris - 1st Carrie E. Hines - Librarian Francis M. Jackson - 10th Herman Jackson - Janitor Tuscan Jasper - 8th, 9th, 10th Alva Johnson - Janitor Lovelena L. Marcus - 9th Blanche G. Moten - 2nd & 3rd Loretta Moten - Clerk Iona Robinson - Substitute Margaree Washington - 6th & 7th Margaret Williams - 5th & 6th	Enrollment 287	Tuition $290.00

Year	Teacher	Enrollment	Notes
1958-1959	Kirk N. Gaskins Sr. - Principal Willis C. Banks - Janitor Edwin K. Barksdale - 9th Ruth Barksdale - 11th Henry M. Brooks Mary L. Byrd Mattie R. Cross - 3rd & 4th Effie M. Davis - 12th Elinora Fowlks - 8th Hester Harris - 1st Francis M. Jackson - 10th Tuscan Jasper - 8th, 9th, 10th Alva Johnson - Janitor Lovelena L. Marcus - 9th Blanche G. Moten - 2nd & 3rd Iona B. Robinson - Substitute Margaree Washington - 6th & 7th Margaret Williams - 5th & 6th	Enrollment 315	Tuition $290.00
1959-1960	Kirk N. Gaskins Sr. - Principal Willis Banks - Janitor Edwin K. Barksdale Henry M. Brooks Mattie R. Cross Effie M. Davis Hester Harris Carrie E. Hines Francis M. Jackson Edna Jasper Tuscan Jasper Alva Johnson Roumaine Lett Lovelena K. Marcus Blanche G. Moten Iona Robinson Gladys Vinson Smith Rev. Milford W. Walker Margaree Washington	Enrollment	Tuition $325.00

Year	Teacher	Enrollment	Notes
1960-1961	Kirk N. Gaskins Sr. - Principal Willis C. Banks - Janitor Edwin K. Barksdale - 9th Henry W. Battle - 8th Social Studies Henry M. Brooks - Industrials Arts Loretta M. Burks - Office Mattie R. Cross - 4th Effie M. Davis - 12th Michael Ford - Athletic Assistant Rosa Francis - 2nd Hester Harris - 1st Edna Jasper - 5th & 6th Tuscan Jasper - 10th & 11th Alva Johnson - Janitor Roumaine Lett - 11th Lovelena L. Marcus - 9th Blanche G. Moten - 3rd Iona B. Robinson - Substitute Gladys V. Smith - 8th Margaree Washington - 6th & 7th Ethel Wheeler -10th	Enrollment 302	Tuition $350.00
1961-1962	Kirk N. Gaskins Sr. - Principal Edwin K. Barksdale - Asst. Principal Willis Banks - Janitor Henry Battle Henry M. Brooks Loretta Burks - Clerk Mary L. Byrd - Migrant Program Mattie R. Cross Effie M. Davis Michael Ford - Athletic Asst. Rosa Francis Hester Harris Carrie E. Hines Francis M. Jackson Edna Jasper Tuscan Jasper Alva Johnson - Janitor Roumaine Lett Lovelena K. Marcus Blanche G. Moten Iona Robinson - Substitute Gladys V. Vinson Margaree Washington Ethel W. Wheeler	Enrollment 335	Tuition $350.00

Year	Teacher	Enrollment	Notes
1963-1964	Kirk N. Gaskins Sr. - Principal Edwin K. Barksdale - Asst. Principal Elizabeth Ashford Willis C. Banks - Janitor Henry W. Battle - 8th Social Studies Henry M. Brooks - Industrials Arts Shirley Bruton Loretta M. Burks - Clerk Mary L. Byrd - Clerk Mattie R. Cross Effie M. Davis Gloria Davis - Substiitute Robert T. Duncan - Elementary Glen L. Gore Hester Harris Roumaine Lett Lovelena L. Marcus Inez Mercer Blanche G. Moten Iona B. Robinson - Sudy Hall Gladys S. Vinson Margaree Washington Ethel W. Wheeler	Enrollment n/a	Tuition $350.00
1964-1965	Kirk N. Gaskins Sr. - Principal Edwin K. Barksdale - Asst. Principal Elizabeth Ashford Willis Banks - Janitor Henry Battle Henry M. Brooks Shirley Bruton Loretta Burks - Clerk Mary L. Byrd - Clerk Mattie R. Cross Effie M. Davis Gloria Davis - Substitute Robert T. Duncan - Elementary Rosa Francis Glen L.Gore Hester Harris Alva Johnson - Janitor Roumaine Lett Lovelena K. Marcus Inez Mercer Blanche G. Moten Iona Robinson - Study Hall Gladys V. Vinson Margaree Washington Ethel W. Wheeler	Enrollment n/a	Tuition $350.00

Year	Teacher	Enrollment	Notes
1965-1966	Kirk N. Gaskins Sr. - Principal	Enrollment n/a	Tuition
	Edwin K. Barksdale - Asst. Principal		
	Elizabeth Ashford		
	Henry W. Battle		
	Henry M. Brooks		
	Shirley Bruton		
	Mary L. Byrd - Clerk		
	Mattie R. Cross		
	Effie M. Davis		
	Gloria Davis - Substiitute		
	Rosa Francis		
	Glen L. Gore		
	Hester Harris		
	Alva Johnson		
	Roumaine Lett		
	Lovelena L. Marcus		
	Inez Mercer		
	Blanche G. Moten		
	Clarence Parnell - Temp Janitor		
	Iona B. Robinson - Sudy Hall		
	Charles Togans - Janitor		
	Gladys S. Vinson		
	Margaree Washington		
	Ethel W. Wheeler		
	Barbara Williams - Elementary		

About the Authors

Judy M. Humbert was born in Winchester, Virginia, and is a member of the 1965 graduating class of Douglas High School. Humbert worked for 35 years for Rubbermaid Commercial Products and for seven years for Southern Scrap. She is a member of Mount Carmel Baptist Church and serves in the deacon/deaconess ministry; she has been chair of the Shepherd's Staff ministry. She has been active in the Black History Task Force, the Douglas Alumni Association (serving as secretary), and the Friends of the Handley Library; she was instrumental in creating the Winchester Black History Heritage Tour. She has served on the boards of the Boys & Girls Clubs, the City Lights Neighborhood Revitalization Program, the Frederick Douglas PTO, and Winchester City Schools. She has been honored with the Peace and Justice Award from the Coalition for Racial Unity, the Ben Belchic Award from Preservation of Historic Winchester, the President's Award for Outstanding Service in Community History from Shenandoah University, and has received the Louis Baker Award from the Winchester-Frederick County Historical Society. Humbert was named a Northern Shenandoah Valley Legend in 2010.

June Gaskins Davis was born in Winchester, Virginia, and is a 1951 graduate of Douglas High School. Her parents were Kirk Gaskins Sr., and Ella Finley Gaskins, who were also born in Winchester. Her father served as principal of Douglas School, 1940–1966. Davis has a B.S. from the University of Maryland, and an M.B.A. from Trinity College. She worked for the federal government and later for Merrill, Lynch, Pierce, Fenner & Smith from which she retired as Assistant Vice President, Financial Consultant. She has lectured, developed seminars, given private speaking engagements, and written articles on finance and investing. The YMCA, Harlem Branch, named her a Black Achiever in Industry. She is a member of the National Association of Women Business Owners, National Black MBA Association, National Council of Career Women, Phi Chi Theta (national fraternity for Women in Business and Economics), Who's Who of American Women, Winchester Business and Professional Women, and Winchester Chamber of Commerce. She is an active member of Mount Carmel Baptist Church. She continues her interests in finance, investing, and local history. She has received the Louis Baker Award from the Winchester-Frederick County Historical Society.

INDEX

Hall, Alice, 26
Hall, Laura, 1
Hall, Laura L.B., 26
Hall, Mary, 26
Hall, Page, 1, 27
Hall, Shirley, 144
Hall, R. Page, 26
Hampden-Sydney, 174
Hampton Institute, 27, 174
Hampton University, 174
Handley High School, 159, 174, 175, 176
Handley Schools, 132
Handley Trustees, 16
Handley, Judge John, 32
Harper, Roland, 20, 23, 138
Harris, Ann, 75
Harris, Audrey, 57, 140
Harris, Beverly Sue, 73, 77, 147
Harris, Bushrod, 77, 87, 148
Harris, Bushrod S., 103
Harris, Charles, 99, 169
Harris, Charles B., 103, 149
Harris, Charles E., 101
Harris, Donte, 176
Harris, Elizabeth, 69
Harris, Hester, 42, 43, 82, 166
Harris, Joseph, 69
Harris, L., 93
Harris, Malissa Elizabeth, 135
Harris, Mary Helen, 153
Harris, Richard, 149
Harris, Richard L., 103
Harris, Sharon Williams, 159, 161, 166, 167, 169
Harris, Shepherd, 99, 103, 167
Harris, Shepherd Jr., 101, 147
Harris, Thelma, 2
Harris, William Shepherd, 101
Haywood, Thomas, 137, 138
Henderson, Emma, 145
Herbert, Amanda, 136
Hines, Carrie, 82
Hofstra, Warren, 165
Hogans, George, 93
Hogans, James, 93
Hogans, Lucille, 3, 132
Hogans, Mary F., 127
Hogans, Mary Frances, 127
Holt, Rev. W.N., 135
Honesty, Lee, 93
Honesty, William, 57, 93
Howard University, 16
Hughes, Smith, 32
Humbert, Andria, 174
Humbert, Judy, 69, 75, 153, 166, 167
Humbert, Sheila D., 151

J

Jackson, 5
Jackson, Adrienne, 176
Jackson, Alberta, 5
Jackson, Amuel W., 133
Jackson, Charles, 51, 55, 78, 95, 97
Jackson, Charles H., 97, 144
Jackson, Chester, 93
Jackson, Colleen, 57, 140
Jackson, Constance, 75
Jackson, Danielle, 174
Jackson, Douglas W., Jr., 175
Jackson, Edward, 69
Jackson, Elizabeth, 72, 146
Jackson, Francis M., 24, 36, 82, 93, 137, 138
Jackson, Frank 77, 148
Jackson, Herman III, 39
Jackson, Herman Jr., 93
Jackson, Herman, III, 150
Jackson, Jerome, 61, 78, 101
Jackson, Joanne, 53
Jackson, Joseph, 103
Jackson, Josephine Randoph, 47, 129, 130, 131
Jackson, Julian Worcester, 47, 130
Jackson, Julian Worchester, 131
Jackson, Lavinia, 53, 153, 154
Jackson, Margaret, 147
Jackson, Mr., 24
Jackson, Pocahontas, 3, 6
Jackson, Preston, 7
Jackson, Robert, 78
Jackson, Sadie, 20
Jackson, Vivienne, 138
Jackson, Wesley, 97
James Madison University, 174, 175
James Wood High School, 176, 177
James, Paul, 7
Jasper, Edna, 42
Jasper, Tuscan, 65, 67, 82, 148
Jenkins, Rev. J. Dallas, 139
Jennings, Helen, 3
Jennings, Madison, 3
John Handley High School, 31
John Mann Methodist Church, 135
Johnson, Emily Page, 135
Johnson, Faye, 57, 140
Johnson, Horace, 49
Johnson, Jacob L., 31
Johnson, Lamont, 99, 101
Johnson, Louis, 97
Johnson, Marlene, 51, 89, 91, 145
Johnson, Monroe, 143
Johnson, Paul, 93
Johnson, Robert Powell, 135
Johnson, Susie, 142
Jones, Rev. Charles A., 147
Jordan, Joy Gaskins, 173

Made in the USA
Middletown, DE
12 January 2015